THE CALEDONIAN CONNECTION

SCOTLAND-RUSSIA TIES —
MIDDLE AGES TO EARLY TWENTIETH
CENTURY

A Concise Biographical List

Dmitry Fedosov

Centre for Scottish Studies
University of Aberdeen

First published 1996
©Centre for Scottish Studies, University of Aberdeen

ISBN 0 906265 22 3

Printed by BPC-AUP Aberdeen Ltd.

Dmitry Gennadevich Fedosov is Research Fellow at the Institute of General History of the Russian Academy of Sciences, and Honorary Research Fellow of the Department of History & Economic History at the University of Aberdeen. His publications include 'The First Russian Bruces', in Grant G. Simpson, ed., *The Scottish Soldier Abroad, 1247-1967*, Edinburgh, 1992; 'Russia's Scottish Clans XVII-XIX Centuries', *J e migrazioni in Europe secc. XIII-XVIII: Atti della 'Venticinquesima Settimana di Studi' 3-8 maggio 1993*, Firenze, 1994; 'A Scottis' Mathematician: Henry Farquharson, c.1675-1739', in Paul Dukes, e⟨ ., *The Universities of Aberdeen and Europe: The First Three Centuries*, Aberdeen, 1995, as well as articles on the Declaration of Arbroath and other subjects in Russian.

The Centre for Scottish Studies in the University of Aberdeen acknowledges with gratitude the financial support given by The Carnegie Trust for the Universities of Scotland towards the costs of production of this publication.

PREFACE

The diverse and fascinating subject of Russo-Scottish connections has not been neglected by historians on either side. However they tended to concentrate on a famous individual like Patrick Gordon, a particular period, for example, the reign of Catherine the Great, or some special aspect such as trade or achievements of Scots doctors in Russia. A.F.Steuart's "Scottish Influences in Russian History" (1913) still remains the only attempt at a general survey.

Some would even regard it as a narrow theme or one not worthy of separate treatment. Professor A.G.Cross (whose work I admire and use in my research) has observed that it is hardly "possible or even meaningful to distinguish Scoto-Russian relations from Anglo-Russian at any period". I believe the distinction is as meaningful as that between Scots and Englishmen themselves.

True, Scots in Russia were and are often dubbed as "anglichane" (a description seldom flattering to the former). All Britons co-existed within the "English" commununity of St. Petersburg or Moscow if only because they were too few to afford separation, and Episcopalians had to share one church with Presbyterians. Nevertheless there were important differences. For instance, until mid-18th century "Russian Scots" were overwhelmingly soldiers while Englishmen mostly engaged in trade. It can also be shown that Scots more readily became Russian citizens and served FOR, rather than IN, their adopted country. There were about a dozen titled Russian families of Scottish descent (Princes Barclay, Counts Bruce, Fermor and Balmain, Barons Stuart, Rutherford and Sutherland etc.) against one English (Barons Dimsdale who never took root in Russia). Among untitled nobility of British extraction Scots prevailed as well. An Englishman remarked in 1805 that "to come from the North side of the Tweed is the best recommendation a man can bring to this city [St.Petersburg], the Caledonian Phalanx being the strongest and most numerous, and moving always in the closest union". It is ironic, but not altogether unjust, that St.Petersburg's English Prospekt was renamed after the Glasgow socialist John Maclean.

Moreover Russo-Scottish ties never quite reached official level, and were less affected by chronic political hostility between London and St.Petersburg. They were contacts between people and cultures, not states and governments, and can thus be called truly interNATIONal. Finally, it is my conviction that in terms of national character Scots have much more in common with us Russians than the English do, and I know this view is shared by many on both sides.

It must be stressed that what follows is merely a draft for a much larger general work I hope to produce eventually, to be titled "Under the Saltire", St.Andrew being, of course, our common Patron. In time my preliminary list will be greatly augmented, new entries added, omissions or mistakes corrected and portraits, pedigrees, coats of arms and other illustrations supplied. I already have at my disposal much more than is offered below. For now, though, only names, dates and brief details of lives and careers are given, with reference to primary or secondary sources in curly brackets. Even so the chronological, geographical and social range of the subject can be appreciated through nearly 400 Scottish names which are recorded (most of them not individuals, but dynasties or "clans"!) from the Middle Ages to around 1920, plus some 60 Russian entries.

I have taken care to select those who are certainly or probably of Scottish birth and ancestry. Fortunately Scots names are often telling. Smiths and Watsons can be a problem, but there is little doubt about characters like Mungo Langcake, Duncan Menzies or Anne Hay Christison.

People on my list fall into five broad categories: 1) Scots who accepted Russian citizenship and settled in the country for good during one or more generations; 2) Scots on temporary service in Russia for periods between several weeks and several decades; 3) British subjects who were active in Russia in some specific role (diplomats, merchants, travellers, missionaries etc.); 4) persons of Scots birth or origin employed by third countries on missions to Russia (as Danish envoy to Muscovy Peter Davidson "de Scotia Aberdonensis", or Spain's first ambassador to St.Petersburg who was a Stuart and a Jacobite). It is not the place here to discuss at any length their fortunes or impact, but they came from all parts of Scotland and took up every conceivable occupation all over the Russian Empire as it was before 1917, from Archangel to the Caucasus, and from Lithuania to Kamchatka. The fifth group are Russian visitors to Scotland, much less numerous, but representing some leading men of our history and culture.

In the long run I would like to see my list as comprehensive as possible and I perfectly realize that I have far to go. Some of the entries deal with noted and well-documented figures, others are just names and dates, but again it is only an outline of the full picture I am working on. Unlike most other writers on the matter I am not content with first- or second-generation Scots. Transition from one nationality to another is always subtle and hard to trace, and it is not easy to say exactly when a Scot turns into a Russian; sometimes it took a few years, sometimes never happened at all. Each case deserves to be considered.

A.F.Steuart once wrote, "Some day a Russian scholar will dig up lists (lists I long to see) of Scottish names from the depths of the archives in Russia. I hope he will come soon". After almost a century it is time to take up the gauntlet. I am much obliged to Professor Paul Dukes of Aberdeen and to my other friends and colleagues in Scotland and at the Moscow Caledonian Club, and to my family, for supporting my quest with unfailing encouragement and sympathy.

Dmitry Fedosov
Moscow, August 1995

ABBREVIATIONS

AK OR	Adres-kalendar'. Obshchaya rospis'
AKV	Arkhiv Kniazia Vorontsova
Alexeyev	M.P.Alexeyev. Russko-angliyskiye literaturnyye sviazi. Moscow, 1982
Bawden, Shamans	C.R. Bawden. Shamans, Lamas and Evangelicals. London,1985
BIHR	Bulletin of the Institute of Historical Research
bp.	baptized
Caledonian Phalanx	The Caledonian Phalanx: Scots in Russia. Edinburgh, 1987
Charykov	N.V.Charykov. Posol'stvo v Rim i sluzhba v Moskve Pavla Meneziya. St.Petersburg, 1906
Cross, By the Banks	A.G. Cross. By the Banks of the Thames: Russians in 18-century Britain. Newtonville, Mass., 1980
DNB	Dictionary of National Biography
Edin.	Edinburgh
f.	fond
IRLI	Institute of Russian Literature, St.Petersburg
L.	London
Lyon Reg.	Public Register of All Arms and Bearings in Scotland. Lyon Office, Edinburgh
M.	Moscow
Moskovsky nekropol'	Moskovsky Nekropol'. 3 vols. St. Petersburg, 1907-8
NLS	National Library of Scotland, Edinburgh
OMS	Obshchy morskoy spisok
op.	opis'
Peterburghsky nekropol'	Peterburgsky nekropol'. 4 vols. St. Petersburg, 1912-3
Phipps	G.M. Phipps. Britons in 17th-century Russia. University of Pennsylvania PhD dissertation, 1971.
P.Gordon, Diary	Diary of Gen.Patrick Gordon of Auchleuchries in RGVIA
PRO	Public Record Office, London

RA	Russky Arkhiv
RBC	Register of British Church, RGIA
RBS	Russky biografichesky slovar'
RGADA	Russian State Archive of Ancient Acts, Moscow
RGAVMF	Russian State Naval Archive, St.Petersburg
RGIA	Russian State Historical Archive, St.Petersburg
RGVIA	Russian State Archive of Military History, Moscow
RIB	Russkaya istoricheskaya biblioteka
RNL	Russian National Library, St.Petersburg
RS	Russkaya Starina
RSL	Russian State Library, Moscow
Sbornik IRIO	Sbornik Imperatorskago Russkago Istoricheskago Obshchestva
Scots in Russia	Scots in Russia 1661-1934. Edinburgh, 1987
Scot.Soldier Abroad	The Scottish Soldier Abroad. Edinburgh & Maryland, USA,1992
SEER	Slavonic and East European Review
Soloviev	S.M. Soloviev. Sochineniya v 18 knigaka. Moscow (in progress)
SRO	Scottish Record Office, Edinburgh
SSR	Scottish Slavonic Review
Stashevsky, Smolenskaya Voyna	E.D. Stashevsky, Smolenskaya Voyna. Kiev, 1919
Steuart	A..F. Steuart. Scottish Influences in Russian History. Glasgow, 1913.
Ustrialov	N.G.Ustrialov. Istoriya tsarstvovaniya Petra Velikago. St.Petersburg, 1853-63

SCOTLAND-RUSSIA TIES – MIDDLE AGES TO EARLY TWENTIETH CENTURY

A CONCISE BIOGRAPHICAL LIST

Dmitry Fedosov

ABERCROMBIE [Аберкромби.Оберкром], JAMES. Captain. 1630s served in Russia under A.Leslie. Went to Britain to hire men for Tsar's service. 14/3/1632 present at muster in Moscow and then at siege of Smolensk. 11/1636 petitioned to leave Muscovy {RGADA, f.150, op.1, 1636, No.4}.

"MARCUS" A. Lieutenant in D.Leslie's company of A.Leslie's regiment. 1632 on muster-roll in Moscow {RGADA, f.210, op.1, No.78}.

JOHN A. 1888 arrived in Tiflis. Wrote "A Trip through the Eastern Caucasus", London, 1889.

ABERDEEN [Абердин], GEORGE HAMILTON GORDON, 4th Earl of (1784-1860). 1804 visited Russia on return from Greece and Asia Minor. British foreign minister and premier. 1844 met Emperor Nicholas I in London. Resigned after outbreak of Crimean War. Helped to publish part of P.Gordon's diary.

ABERNETHY [Абернети], JAMES. 1660s colonel in Russian army {P.Gordon, Diary}.

ADAIR, Sir ROBERT (1763-1855). Son of King George III's surgeon. M.P. 1791 came to St.Petersburg during the "Ochakov Crisis" as an emissary of the Whigs who opposed Pitt's anti-Russian course. Favourably received by Empress Catherine II {A. Cunningham, "Robert Adair's mission to St.Petersburg", BIHR, No.132, 1982}.

ADAMSON [Адамсон], JAMES. Served in Russian army in 17th century {RIB, XXVIII}.

WILLIAM A. 1737-1762 officer in Russian Navy {OMS, II}.

ADIE [Flbt], JOHN.   Private of   A.Annand's company in A.Leslie's regiment.   1632 appears in Moscow and probably fought in Smolensk War {RGADA, f.210, op.1, No.78, f.21}.

AFFLECK [Афлек], JAMES.   Lieutenant.   1632 appears on muster-roll in Moscow as "unassigned" to any regiment, but probably fought at Smolensk.   Was paid 12,5 roubles a month {RGADA, f.210, op.1, No.78, f.53}.

AGATHA (ca.1025-1070x).   Relative of Queen Ghisela of Hungary where she married English Prince Edward "The Exile".   She had an Orthodox name and probably came from Russian princely dynasty of Kiev,closely connected with Western Europe and Hungary in particular. Her children were Edgar Etheling and St.Margaret of Scotland.   1068 Agatha and her family fled from the Normans to Scotland and she must have died there after Margaret wedded Malcolm III, King of Scots. {V.I.Matuzova. Angliyskiye Srednevekovyye Istochniki. Moscow, 1979, pp.38-9, 58-9; G.W.S. Barrow. Scotland: Kingship and Unity, p.29).

AIKMAN [Аикман,Акман], ADAM.   Army officer in 17th-century Muscovy {RIB, XXVIII}.
JOHN A. (+1773).   1771 enlisted as lieutenant in Russian Navy {OMS, II}.

AIRTH [Эрт,Ерт], WALTER (+1678).   Captain.   1661 left Swedish service for that of Russia on advice of P.Gordon and with testimonials from Swedish Field Marshal Douglas and an English general. Later infantry major.
Ensign DANIEL A.(son of above?) 1698 took part in battle against Streltsy rebels near Voskresensky monastery. {RGADA, f.150, op.1, 1661, No.23; P.Gordon, Diary; N.Ustrialov. Istoriya tsarstvovaniya Petra Velikago, III, p.582-3}.

ALEXANDER [Александер], JAMES.   1690s colonel of Russian army {P.Gordon, Diary}.
WILLIAM A. 1730s-40s dyer in St.Petersburg. Nephew or cousin of H.Farquharson whose sole heir he became {F.Veselago.Ocherk istorii morskogo kadetskogo korpusa. St.Pb., 1852, p.102}.

Sir JAMES EDWARD A. (1803-1885). Traveller and soldier. 1829 came to Russia and accompanied her army on campaign against Turks. Published his "Travels to the Seat of War in the East through Russia and the Crimea", L.,1830. 1854 witnessed the siege of Sevastopol.

ALEXANDRA [Александра Фёдоровна] (1872, Darmstadt-1918, Yekaterinburg). Princess Alix of Hesse-Darmstadt, grand-daughter of Queen Victoria. From 1894 Russian Empress, wife of Nicholas II. 9/1896 visited Scotland and stayed at Balmoral with her husband and infant daughter Olga. Killed by Bolsheviks {Dnevniki Imperatora Nikolaya II. Moscow, 1991, pp.167-70}.

ALLAN [Аллен], EDWARD and JOHN 1632 privatos in A.Leslie's regiment {RGADA, f.210, op.1, No.78}.
Sir WILLIAM A. (1782, Edinburgh-1850, ibid.). Painter. Stayed and worked in Russia 1805-14, 1841 and 1844, learned Russian and travelled to Ukraine, Caucasus etc. Some of his works were acquired by Emperor Nicholas I and are preserved in Russian collections. Became president of Royal Scottish Academy {DNB, I, 297-8}.

ANDERSON [Андерсон]. 1632 several Andersons served in Muscovy under A.Leslie who were either Scottish or Scandinavian.
ALEXANDER MAGNUS A. Swedish major of Scottish descent. 1712 went over to Russians, but then sent to Siberia. {Steuart, 84}.
GEORGE A. 1714-21 lieutenant in Russian Navy, commanded a boat at Riga.
PETER A. (+1770x). 1736 joined Russian Navy as lieutenant. Fought in Baltic campaigns against Sweden and in Seven Years' War. Director of Admiralty Office, commander-in-chief at Kronshtadt and Reval. 1769 vice-admiral. {OMS}.

ANDREWS [Андрус], IAN. 1632 soldier in A.Annan's company of A.Leslie's regiment.
DAVID A. also served in Tsar's army in 17th century {RIB, XXVIII}.

ANNAN [Аннан(д)], ALEXANDER. Captain. 1631 hired by A.Leslie and commanded 3rd company of his regiment. Apparently distinguished himself in Smolensk War; lieutenant-colonel by 1633.

JOHN ANNAND. 1660s surgeon in Moscow {RGADA, f.150 & f.210, op.1, No.78; P.Gordon, Diary}.

ANNENKOV [Анненков], PAVEL VASILYEVICH (1812, Moscow-1887, Dresden). Writer, publisher and critic. 1843 visited Scotland and briefly recorded his impressions (unpublished). 1871 helped I.S.Turgenev to prepare his speech for Sir Walter Scott's jubilee in Edinburgh. {IRLI, St.Petersburg; P.V.Annenkov. Parizhskiye pis'ma. M., 1983, pp.449, 556}.

ARBUTHNOT, ANDREW (1606, Scotland-1684, Kiev). Possibly a merchant trading in Poland and Russia. P.Gordon wrote an epitaph for him: "Scotia me genuit tenuitque Polonia quondam, Russia nunc requiem praebet. Amice, vale" {P.Gordon, Diary}.

ALEXANDER A. buried at St.Petersburg 2/5/1759.

THOMAS A. Merchant. Buried St.Petersburg 13/1/1761 {RBC}.

GENERAL A. of British army. Fought in American and French wars. 1839 visited Russia and was entertained at Imperial estate of Ropsha near St.Petersburg {Rossiya pervoy poloviny XIX veka glazami inostrantsev, 1991, p.693}.

ARMSTRONG [Армстронг], ADAM (1762, Gavish near Jedburgh-1818, Petrozavodsk). Educated for ministry, but went to Russia in early 1780s as tutor to the Greig family. Later an assistant of C.Gascoigne whom he succeeded as director of Olonets factories in 1807. Became Russian citizen and Marshal of the Olonets nobility. He married twice and had children including

ROBERT [Роман Адамович] A. (1791-1865, St.Petersburg). Studied at Edinburgh. 1811 returned to Russia to serve with his father at Olonets works. 1843-58 directed St.Petersburg Mint and became Lt.-Gen. of Engineers. {RGIA, f.1343, op.16, No.2693 & f.1689}.

JOHN [Иван Адамович] A. (*1807). 1843 = Baroness Adelaide Rosen.

ARNOT(T) [Арнот], JOHN. Officer in Muscovite army, 17th century {RIB, XXVIII}.

JOHN A. Travelled to St.Petersburg in early 19th century and may have supplied material for W.Godwin's novel "Cloudsley" (1830) {G.Woodcock. William Godwin. A Biographical Study. L., 1956, P.230}.

AUCHTERLONY [Охтерлони, Ухтерлоне]. Scots officer JAMES "AKHTONLONI" mentioned in 17th-century Russian pay registers {RIB, XXVIII}.

ROBERT "OUCHTERLONY" +25/1/1830, St.Petersburg, aged 75.

Lt.-Gen. ALEXANDER ROMANOVICH O. (son of above?) +1860,Moscow. His son was

Capt. ALEXANDER O. (1830-1893). Both were buried in Moscow, and other members of the family near St.Petersburg. 1917 their Scottish kinsmen made fruitless inquiries about them for the name was misread by Russian officials as "Ukhterlong"! {RGIA, f.1689, No.2 & f.1343, op.37, No.30587}.

AULD. In Russia from 1790s. MARGARET, wife of ROBERT A. +1798, St.Petersburg, aged 22.

THOMAS A.+1823, St.Petersburg, aged 50. His children were born in Russian capital {RBC}.

BAILLIE [Белли], THOMAS. 1660s colonel in Russia. 1670 commanded a unit at Astrakhan besieged by Razin's rebel cossacks and evidently lost his life there {RGADA, f.150, op.1, 1660, No.4; Soloviev, VI, 291-3}.

Judging by their coat of arms the Russian noble family of B. was related to the senior branch of Lamington. HENRY [Григорий Григорьевич] B. (ca.1762-1826, Nikolayev) 1783 left British Navy for Russia as midshipman. 1799 capt. of 2nd rank in Mediterranean expedition. His surprise capture of Naples from the French with a small force prompted Emperor Paul's remark, "B. wished to amaze me, and I will amaze him", which meant a star of St.Anne, 1st class. 1816 he became rear-admiral in command of a Black Sea naval division {OMS}.

WILLIAM [Василий Васильевич] B. (1769, Edinburgh-1827, Archangel). Engineer. Related to the above and grandson of "Gen.Sir Evan B.,Bart.,British commander in Bengal". Director of Shirshim works at Archangel, state councillor and knight of St.Vladimir, 4th class. He left a big family, and his eldest son ALEXANDER (1800-1872) was a major-gen. {Memoirs of V.A.Belli, unpublished}.

Other Baillies lived in St.Petersburg since 1780s including a builder apparently associated with C.Cameron, and CHARLOTTE B. was mother of famous Russian liberal K.D. Kavelin {RBC}.

BAIN [Баи]. 1660 JEREMY "BAN", major of the Austrian army, came to Archagel to serve the Tsar "perpetually". 1695 Colonel JAMES "BANE" was killed at the siege of Azov. Both could have been Scottish {RGADA, f.150, op.1, 1660, No.3; P.Gordon, Diary}.

1811 JAMES BAIN = Marie Du Roveray at St.Petersburg and had a daughter, FANNY .

DANIEL B. +1854, St.Petersburg, aged 60 {RBC}.

BAIRD [Берд], JOHN. Stonemason. 1784, aged 25, came to Russia to work under C.Cameron. {A.G. Cross, "Charles Cameron's Scottish Workmen", SSR, No.10, 1988}.

CHARLES [Карл Николаевич] B. (1766, Westertown near Carron-1843, St.Petersburg). Son of Superintendent of Forth & Clyde Canal. 1786 moved to Russia with C.Gascoigne; 1792 established his own foundry, the first in St.Petersburg. Also ran a wharf, saw-mill, flour-mill and sugar refinery. Constructed bridges and machines for the Mint and

Arsenal. 1815 built Russia's earliest steamship, "Yelizaveta", and obtained shipping monopoly on the Neva and Gulf of Finland. He was assisted by his brothers JAMES and NICOL (1779-1812) and succeeded by his son FRANCIS (1802-1864) and grandson GEORGE (*1842). Huge reliefs and statues for St.Isaac's Cathedral, Alexander Column etc. in St.Petersburg and carriage for Tsar Cannon in Moscow Kremlin were cast at Baird's works. Leading industrialists in their adopted country, the Bairds won many decorations, took Russian citizenship and were ennobled. {RGIA, f.1343, op.17, No.3034 & f.1689; Caledonian Phalanx, 69-75}.

BAKHMETEV [Бахметев],YURY ALEXEYEVICH (*ca.1760). Studied in Moscow and London. 1780 began courses in Edinburgh University under W.Cullen. Received MD from Edinburgh (his thesis was called "De variolis inserendis") and MA from St.Andrews. Member of Medical and Natural History Societies of Edinburgh and of the Royal College of Physicians. 1787 returned to Russia, but did not pursue a medical career. {AKV; Cross, By the Banks, 139-40, 145}.

BAKUNIN [Бакунин], PAVEL PETROVICH (1762-1805). Nephew of Count S.Vorontsov, Russian Ambassador to Britain. 1785-7 studied at Edinburgh University. Corresponding member of Society of Antiquaries of Scotland and member of Natural History Society where he read a paper "On the Means Used by Nature for the Preservation of Vegetables from the Effects of Cold during the Winter in High Lattitudes". 1794 B. succeeded his aunt Princess Dashkova as Director of St.Petersburg Academy of Sciences and President of Russian Academy ensuring nomination of Dugald Stewart as honorary member of the former. {AKV; Cross, By the Banks, 142-3}.

BALFOUR [Бальфур], JAMES. Scion of Balfours of Pittendreich and Monvanie, eldest son of John B. of Edinburgh, younger brother of James, 1st of Pilrig. Ca.1770 founded a trading house in Riga and became a Russian subject. His son and heir
JOHN LEWIS B. "1st Guild" merchant and "honorary citizen". 1842 received his pedigree and coat of arms from Lyon Office and petitioned Russian Senate to recognize him as hereditary nobleman which was refused because he did not attain the ranks or decorations required. He

married a niece of Prince <u>M.B.Barclay de Tolly</u>, and his eldest son engaged in medicine {RGIA, f.1343, op.17, No.709 & op.39, No.296}.

BALLACH [Балач,Балака], WILLIAM. 1785 midshipman in Russian Navy. 1789 captured by Swedes in the Baltic, but freed in a year and promoted to lieutenant. 1808 dismissed after Russia broke relations with Britain {OMS, III}.

BALLANTINE [Баленштейн], ARCHIBALD. 1703 enlisted in Russian Navy as lieutenant. 1704 served on a ship built on the Sias' river. {OMS, I}.

BALMAIN [Де бальмен], COUNTS of. Branch of clan <u>Ramsay</u> named after a barony in Kincardine. DEODATUS [Богдан] CHARLES ADRIAN de B. (+1741), whose father left Scotland after "Glorious Revolution", stayed in France and possibly Turkey. 1736 entered Russian service as major, then colonel of 2nd Moscow regt. Killed at the storming of Vilmanstrand during war with Sweden. His son
ANTHONY CHRISTOPHER (1740-1790), lt.-gen. 1768-1774 fought in Turkish war. Russian Envoy in the Crimea, Director of Land Cadet Corps, Governor-Gen. of Orel and Kursk, Commander-in-Chief in the Caucasus, where he died. Had two daughters and three sons:
ALEXANDER CHARLES ADEODATUS (1779-1848). Major-gen. Took part in Russo-French and Turkish wars, served with Russian missions in Italy, Austria and Britain. 1815-20 Russian representative at St.Ielena where Napoleon was confined. 1822-6 with Russian embassy in London; King George IV often asked him, "Eh bien,Balmain, quand donc irez vous visiter vos cousins en Ecosse?" His brother CHARLES (1784-1812), major-gen. at 24, died of wounds during the French invasion.
Although their rights to the comital title are unclear, it was finally confirmed by the Emperor in 1845, and the family survived into 20th century. {RGIA, f.1343, op.46, No.1167; RA, 1868}.

BALOBANOVA [Балобанова], YEKATERINA VIACHES-LAVOVNA (1847-1927). Writer and translator. Studied Celtic languages in France and Germany. 1879 stayed in Scotland working in archives of Aberdeen and Edinburgh. Translated Ossian into Russian {Panteon Literatury, 1890 & 1897}, wrote articles,essays and children's stories on

Scottish and Celtic subjects {Shotlandiya.Iz let daliokikh. St.Petersburg, 1913 etc.}.

BANNATINE, JAMES. Captain. 10/1632 arrived in Moscow with recommendations to Tsar Mikhail from King Charles I and Prince of Orange, but was not accepted for Russian service on the pretext that Tsar's title was incomplete in Prince's letter {Phipps, pp.270, 282, 296-7}.

BANNERMAN. 12/1661 a girl of that name, probably daughter of a Scots officer, married a Capt. Lome in Moscow's Foreign Quarter.{Gordon, Diary}.

BANNISTER. Family appears in St.Petersburg ca.1800. THOMAS, son of JOHN B. was born and died in Russian capital 3/1804 {RBC}.

BARATYNSKY [Баратынский], BOGDAN ANDREYEVICH. Vice-admiral. 1799 led a Russian squadron from Archangel to North Sea to join forces with the British against the French. His brother ILYA, capt. of 2nd rank, commanded the ship "Yaroslav". After suffering in a storm in October the squadron wintered in Scotland {OMS, III; E.Turner, "Russian Squadron with Admiral Duncan's North Sea Fleet", Mariner's Mirror, XLIX, 1963}.

BARCLAY De TOLLY [Барклай де Толли]. 1621 Peter B., merchant and kinsman of Sir Patrick B. of Towie, left Banff for Rostock. 1664 his son JOHN STEPHEN, a lawyer, settled in Riga and was still alive when Russians conquered Livonia in 1710.

The name was immortalized in Russian history by MICHAEL [Михаил Богданович] B. de TOLLY (1757-1818). Son of a humble army lieutenant, he started as a cuirassier N.C.O. and could rely only on his own talents. Excelling in almost every campaign since Russo-Turkish war of 1787-91 he became first Russian Governor-Gen. of Finland and as Minister of War reformed Russian army. 1812, in command against the invading French, he was much maligned for his unpopular (but only possible) retreat strategy. 1813 B. led the Russo-Prussian forces in Europe and was in charge of the allies' centre at the battle of Leipzig. He went on to conquer Paris and win the rank of Field Marshal and Prince of the Russian Empire. {RGVIA; M.Josselson. The Commander:A Life of Barclay de Tolly. Oxford, 1980}. The title was inherited by his grand-nephew, ALEXANDER B.de TOLLY-WEYMARN.

Another branch stemmed from the Prince's cousin, AUGUST B., Burgomaster of Riga. His sons GEORG, AUGUST and JOHANN were created Russian noblemen in 1827.

IVAN B. (1811-1879), a doctor at Piatigorsk, issued a death certificate when the poet M.Lermontov was killed in a duel.

Russian Barclays were Lutheran, but ARTHUR B. and his family attended British Church in St.Petersburg in 1820s {RBC, II}.

BAXTER [Бакстер,Бякстер], ALEXANDER (ca.1730-1803x). Merchant, member of Russia Company. 1773 appointed Russia's first Consul-Gen. in Britain, a post he still held in 1800s, and contributed in many ways to Russo-British contacts. 1803 made Councillor of Russian College of Commerce {AKV; V.N. Aleksandrenko. Russkiye diplo-maticheskiye agenty v Londone. Warsaw, 1897}.

JAMES [Яков Николаевич] B. (1789, Scotland-1855x). Claimed to belong to Clan Buchanan. Studied at Edinburgh and fought in French wars. 1821 moved to Russia and launched the important but short-lived "English Literary Journal of Moscow" for which he wrote "Biographical Sketch of Sir Walter Scott" etc. Taught English at Moscow University and privately. Became Russian subject, State Councillor and Director of St.Petersburg Commercial Institute. 1841 married Charlotte Ross and had issue. {RGIA, f. 1343, op.17, No.7713 & f.1689, No.3; The Journals of Claire Clairmont. Cambridge, Mass., 1968}.

BEATON [Битон], ACHILLES. Lieutenant. 1632 present at muster of A.Leslie's regiment in Moscow and had monthly salary of 12,5 roubles {RGADA, f.210, op.1, No.78, f.53}.

1815 WILLIAM "BEETON" married Ann Lockhart in St.Petersburg {RBC, II}.

BEATTIE, ROBERT. Bricklayer. 1784 came to St.Petersburg, aged 29, as one of C.Cameron's craftsmen. {A.Cross in SSR, No.10, 1988}.

BELIAYEV [Беляев], NIKOLAY IVANOVICH (ca.1760-1803x). Cadet at Naval Corps. 1774 along with S.I.Rachinsky and I.N.Shishukov came to Edinburgh to study at University under J.Robison, Dugald Stewart and Adam Ferguson. 1777 returned to teach French at Naval Corps. Translated J.Black's lectures. Freemason. {Cross, By the Banks, pp.129-31}.

BELL [Беллъ], JOHN (1691, Antermony, Stirlingshire-1780, ibid.). Doctor, traveller and diplomat. 1714 entered Russian service with help from R.Erskine. Took part in Russian missions to Persia (1715-8) and China (1719-21) and Peter the Great's Caspian expedition (1722). 1734, after a spell at home, returned to St.Petersburg as secretary to British Minister. 1739-40 British charge d'affaires in Russia. He married a Russian and took her back to his estate. Wrote "Travels from St.Petersburg in Russia to Diverse Parts of Asia", 2 vols., Glasgow, 1763, also published in France, Russia and Germany.

There were many other BELLS in St.Petersburg and Moscow from 18th to early 20th century {RBC}.

ROBERT B. C.Cameron's bricklayer. 1784 in Russia, aged 40 {SSR, No.10, 1988}.

JOHN B. 1789 lieutenant in Russian Navy. 1790 captured by Swedes {OMS, III}.

JAMES STANISLAUS B. Merchant of Dundee, brother of the artist John Z.Bell. 1836 his ship was detained by Russians in Black Sea and he spent some time in the country. Wrote "Journal of a Residence in Circassia during the Years 1837, 1838 and 1839", 2 vols., L., 1840.

BERVIE [Берви], WILLIAM [Василий Федорович] (1793-1859). Son of British Consul in Danzig. Became Russian citizen and professor of medicine at Kazan University. His son was

VASILY B.-FLEROVSKY (1829-1918), noted socialist and economist {RGIA, f.1343, op.17, No.2987}.

BERWICK [Бервик,Бервиц]. Descendants of James Stewart, Duke of Berwick (1670-1734), natural son of King James VII (II). They settled in Russia and claimed baronial title {RGIA, f.1343, op.46, Nos. 1695-6}. Cf. Liria.

BISSET [Биссет], JAMES. One of six granite-masons from Kemnay, Aberdeenshire, who worked in Odessa. 1869, after over two years there, he and family were allegedly ordered out of Russia because he held a prohibited edition of Burns' poems, and walked 3,000 miles back home in 14 months! His son was known as "The Russian" among villagers. {The Scotsman Weekend, 19/1/1991}.

ALEXANDER B. (*1854, Inverurie). Aberdeen graduate. Studied tea planting in India. 1893 came to Russia, was soon given charge of Imperial tea plantations in Georgia and published "Practical Manual on Tea-Planting and Manufacture". Lived in Batum.

BODIE [Боде,Боди], JAMES (+1780,Russia). 1770 joined Russian Navy as capt.-lt. and commanded a vessel at the battle of Cesme. 1777 capt.of 2nd rank. ANN B., who died at St.Petersburg in 1826, aged 76, possibly was his widow {OMS, III; RBC, II}.

BOGDANOVICH [Богданович], PIOTR IVANOVICH (ca.1748-1803). Writer and publisher, son of a Ukrainian landowner. 1760s studied at Leipzig and probably Glasgow. 1771 back in Russia. 1787 set up a private print in St.Petersburg. {RNL, f.341, No.385; Cross, By the Banks, 292}.

BONAR [Бонар],THOMSON. From 1770s prominent merchant in London and St.Petersburg. His son THOMSON was born in Russian capital in 1780 and married Anastasia Jessy Gascoigne nee Guthrie in 1807 {RBC}.

BORTHWICK [Бордовик,Бортвиг], FIODOR MATVEY-EVICII. 1690s major of 1st Moscow regt. 18/6/1698 took part in battle against Streltsy rebels at Voskresensky monastery. Then colonel {P.Gordon, Diary}.

GEORGE JOHN ROBERT [Роман Иванович] B. (ca. 1768, Scotland-1827, Archangel). Capt. of 1st rank. 1788 midshipman in Russia. 15/7/1789 fighting the Swedes at Oland he was badly wounded by a cannon blast and then introduced to the Empress who found him handsome apart from red hair. After Mediterranean campaigns of 1805-8 received golden sword for bravery and order of St.George,4th class. {OMS, III, pp.207-9}.

BOWER ST.CLAIR, ALEXANDER. Grandson of the Jacobite B. of Kincaldrum who went to France. After service in India married Countess Kosakowska and lived on her estate in Lithuania which he described in his letters (1845-72). {A.F.Steuart. Papers Relating to Scots in Poland.Edin., 1915, p.115}.

BOWIE, ROBERT. 29/8/1771 married Henrietta Stuart in St.Petersburg. Their daughter MARTHA born there same year {RBC, I}.

BOYD [бойд], THOMAS. Lieutenant. 1647 arrived to enter Russian service with Col. Urie and others {RGADA, f.150, op.1, 1647, No.27}.

BROUN [броун], DAVID and JOHN. Scots officers in Muscovite army in 17th century {RIB, XXVIII}. Several more Brouns, including Ruitmaster HENRY, appear on muster-roll of 1632.

BRUCE [брюс], ANDREW. 1632 corporal in A.Gordon's company of A.Leslie's regt. {RGADA, f.210, op.1, No.78}.
    WILLIAM B. (ca.1625-1680). Of Clackmannan branch. 1647 joined Tsar's army as ensign. Fought and wounded in Polish and Swedish wars. 1658 colonel. Married widow of Col.Inglis. Their children were Robert, James and Elizabeth.
    ROBERT [Роман Вилимович] (1668-1720, St.Petersburg). Active in Crimean and Azov campaigns. 1700 colonel. 1704 first High Commandant of St.Petersburg, directly responsible for construction and defence of the city. Repulsed several Swedish attacks on it. 1710 besieged Viborg and seized Kexholm, made lt.-gen. 1719 member of War College. Founded first Evangelical church of St.Anne in the capital. Buried near SS.Peter and Paul's Cathedral. Had nine children including ALEXANDER (1704-1760), lt.-gen. and heir of his uncle, ELIZABETH DOROTHY and MARY , who married the Fermor brothers.
    JAMES DANIEL [Яков Вилимович] (1669, Moscow-1735, Glinki). General, statesman, diplomat and scholar, one of closest advisors of Peter the Great. 1686 cavalry cornet. Took part in Crimean and Azov expeditions. 1698 studied in Britain, became Russia's earliest Newtonian, on return established first observatory in the country. 1700 major-gen.;

commanded and reformed artillery in Great Northern War as Master of the Ordnance. 1709 got Order of St.Andrew for his decisive role at Poltava. 1712-3 headed allied artillery of Russia,Denmark and Poland-Saxony in Pomerania and Holstein. 1717 senator and President of Colleges of Mines and Manufacture; also in charge of Moscow print and St.Petersburg mint. First Minister plenipotentiary at Aland and Nystad congresses, negotiated and signed peace treaty with Sweden in 1721 when he became Count of Russian Empire. 1726 retired with rank of field marshal. Known as the most enlightened man in Russia, he possessed a rich library in 14 languages, and collection of "curiosities". B. took pride in Scottish ancestry and corresponded with his Jacobite kinsmen. {D.Fedosov, "The First Russian Bruces" in The Scottish Soldier Abroad, Edin.& Maryland, 1992, pp.55-66}. Line extinct 1829, but there were others.

JOHN B. 1664 delivered a letter from King Charles II to the Tsar asking to release Generals <u>Dalyell</u> and <u>Drummond</u> from his employ.

Major JAMES B. died at siege of Azov 1695 {P.Gordon, Diary}.

PETER HENRY B. (1692, Detring, Westphalia-1757 near Cupar, Fife). Engineer-capt., related to Russian Bruces. 1711-24 served in Russia. Went on mission to Constantinople, taught fortification to Grand Duke Peter and saw action against Turkey, Sweden and Persia. Produced an early map of Caspian Sea. Wrote "Memoirs of P.H.Bruce, A Military Officer in the Services of Prussia,Russia and Gr.Britain", L., 1782.

HENRY B. (1700-1772), nephew of Laird of Clackmannan and last of his line, came to Russia 1720 with two JAMES BRUCES and enlisted ensign in Russian army {SRO, Airth Writs, GD 37/328-9}.

ANN B. (1691-1780). 1726 married Ludowick Lobrey in St. Petersburg , and died there. {RBC, I}.

WILLIAM B. 1774 came from Carron with a party of engineers to install a steam-powered water-pump in Kronshtadt dock. Became Russian citizen and trained local workers. {Caledonian Phalanx, p.65}.

CHARPENTIER B., a "Swede"(!), served as capt.-lt. in Black Sea 1791. {OMS, III}.

BRUNNOW [брунноб], FILIPP IVANOVICH (1797, Dresden-1875, Darmstadt). Baron and Count. 1840-54 and 1858-74 Russian Ambassador in Britain. Visited Scotland, notably in 1847 when he accompanied Grand Duke <u>Constantine</u> to Blair Atholl. {TsGAVMF, f.224, op.1, Nos.5,7}.

BRUNTON [Брунтон], Rev. HENRY (+1813, Karras). Native of Selkirk. Member of Edinburgh Missionary Society. 1802 a founder of Scottish missionary settlement ("Shotlandka") at Karras in North Caucasus. First translator of New Testament into "Tatar-Turkish" language, published 1813 and 1818. {Caledonian Phalanx, pp.75-7}.

BRYCE or BRICE, GEORGE. Stonemason. 1784 came to Russia to work under <u>C.Cameron</u>.
MARGARET B. married architect <u>W.Hastie</u> in St.Petersburg 1795 and died at Tsarskoye Selo 1847 {SSR, No.10, 1988; RBC}.

BRYDONE, PATRICK (1736, Coldingham-1818, Lennel House, Berwickshire). Traveller and writer. 1776 came to St.Petersburg via Warsaw and Riga. Spent a month there and wrote a diary (unpublished). {Caledonian Phalanx, p.38; DNB, III, p.166-7}.

BUCHAN. 1680s colonel of Russian army serving in Ukraine {P.Gordon, Diary}.

BUCHANAN, JAMES (1791-1868). Born Pennsylvania of Scottish parents. 1831-3 American Minister in St.Petersburg. 1832 concluded Russo-American trade treaty, in force until 1911. 1857-61 US president.
ANDREW B. (1807-1882, Milngavie). Son of James B. of Blairvadoch and a daughter of Earl of Caithness. On diplomatic service in many countries. Spent several terms in St.Petersburg: 1838-41 attache, 1844-51 secretary and charge d'affaires, 1864-71 ambassador. 1878 retired and created bart. His son
Sir GEORGE WILLIAM B. (1854-1924). Last British ambassador in Russian Empire 1910-17. Opposed Bolsheviks and recalled 1918. Wrote "My Mission to Russia and Other Diplomatic Memories", 1923.

BURNES [Бэрнес]. Taught English at St.Petersburg. 1907-8 among his pupils was Vladimir Nabokov who acquired fluency in the language. The Russian writer later learned that "the bright-eyed Scot" who seemed an ordinary tutor was also a translator of Russian verse "most esteemed by Edinburgh experts". {V.Nabokov. Drugiye berega. Ann Arbor, 1978, pp.77-84}.

BURNETT [Барнет. Борнет], ANDREW. Son of a Thomas B. 1661 joined Russian service from that of Poland as lieutenant along with other Scots. Friend of P.Gordon who once saved him from fighting a duel. Colonel by 1678 when he took part in Chigirin campaign receiving several light wounds in battle with Turks on the Dnieper {RGADA, f.150, op.1, 1661, No.33; P.Gordon, Diary}.

CAIRNS, ROBERT. Lived in St.Petersburg, where he married Elizabeth Twycross, widow, 1803, and in Moscow. Their Russian-born daughters appear in St.Petersburg 1828. {RBC}.

CAITHNESS [Катнес], WILLIAM. (+1772). 1715 boatswain in Russian Navy. 1720 skipper, then rigging master in Kronshtadt. 1733 lieutenant, served in the Admiralty. 1754 capt. of 3rd rank. 1762 retired. Married thrice. {OMS, I; RBC, I}.

CALDER, GEORGE. 1822 married Barbara Bailey, St.Petersburg. Their son CHARLES born 1824. {RBC, II}.

CALDERWOOD [Кальдервуд], ANDREW. (+1692,Moscow). 1661 one of some 30 Scots officers who after meeting P. Gordon in Riga left Swedish service for Russia and enlisted in D. Crawford's regt. 1680s major, then colonel. Had a daughter. {P. Gordon, Diary}.
DAVID C. 1714-5 officer in Russian Navy. {OMS, I}.
LEWIS C. (+1755). 1728 in Russia as surgeon to Preobrazhensky Guards. Also worked in Moscow and St.Petersburg hospitals until he died. {Steuart, p.114}.

CAMERON [Камерон], CHARLES [Карл Карлович] (+19/3/1812, St.Petersburg, aged 66; the year of his birth is thus 1745 or 6). One of the greatest Scottish architects, although he built only in Russia after a spell in Italy where he wrote "Baths of the Romans", L., 1772. 1779 he came to St.Petersburg stressing his clan's Jacobite connections and was appointed Empress Catherine's architect. He invited several dozen Scottish stonemasons, bricklayers and smiths to assist him, some of whom embarked on careers of their own, as Wilsons, A.Menelaws and W.Hastie. His celebrated works are to be seen in Tsarskoye Selo (interiors of Great Palace, "Cameron Gallery", Cold Baths, St.Sophia's Cathedral etc.) and Pavlovsk (Palace and park pavilions) as well as in Ukraine (Razumovsky palace, Baturin). 1802-5 C. was employed by the Admiralty and made designs for its main building in St.Petersburg and St.Andrew's Cathedral in Kronshtadt, used by his successor A.Zakharov. {V.N.Taleporovsky. Charles Cameron. Moscow, 1939; A.G.Cross in SSR, No.10, 1988}.

His brother or nephew WALTER C. was merchant in St.Petersburg from 1780s to 1816.

CAMPBELL [Кампбель]. 1660s capt. in D.Crawford's regt. of Tsar's army. 1690s colonel. {P. Gordon, Diary}.

JAMES C. Colonel of Russian dragoons. 28/9/1708 distinguished in battle with Swedes at Lesnaya, promoted to brigadier, but soon back in Britain. Corresponded with R.Erskine. {A. Gordon, History of Peter the Great, I, pp.274-5, 292}. He may have been Sir James C. of Lawers (1667-1745), third son of 3rd Earl of Loudoun, lt.-gen. and MP.

ALEXANDER C. (1760-1802, St.Petersburg). 1784 came to Russia as C.Cameron's stonemason,aged 23. 1791 announced in St.Petersburg paper that his wife Nancy ran away. She left for home,but he was still employed by Russian Palace Office. {SSR, No.10, 1988, p.64; RBC, I}.

JOHN FRANCIS C. of Islay (1822-1885). Expert on Gaelic language and culture. 1873-4 traversed Russia from White to Black Sea calling at Archangel, Yaroslavl, Astrakhan and other cities. Made sketches and compiled a diary {2 Journal of "Travels in Norway, Russia and Italy" in NLS, Adv. MSS 50.4.8.}.

CARMICHAEL [Кармихель], JOHN (16th cent.). Of Howgate near Edinburgh, uncle to Sir John C. of Hyndford, Warden of the March. "General" under Ivan the Terrible. 1570 in command of 5,000 men during Livonian War and later became Governor of Pskov. {Steuart, 19-20}.

MUNGO C. (+x1662). Lieutenant hired by A.Leslie in 1631. Colonel by 1650 when he was sent with Col.Hamilton and 4,000 infantry to quell a mutiny at Pskov. {Olearius}.

On Leslie's muster-roll in Moscow in 1632 there were Ensign WILLIAM, "Sub-Ruitmasters" ALEXANDER and WALTER and Corporal JOHN C., last two in the company of Capt. RICHARD C., who as major was expelled from Russia with his family in 1642 for conspiring to murder Dyak Vasily Rtishchev. {RGADA, f.210, op.1, No.78 & f.150, op.1, 1642, No.4}.

Col. MARTIN C. mentioned in Russian service 1649-54.

ARCHIBALD C. (+7/8/1695). Died of wounds at siege of Azov, Catholic convert. {P. Gordon, Diary}.

Cf. Hyndford.

CARNEGIE [Карнеги], JOHN. 1720s shipmaster of Montrose who traded at Riga. 1724 he took P.H.Bruce back to Scotland on board the "Isabella". {Memoirs of P.P.Bruce, p.367}.

ELIZABETH C. (1750-1793). Married Lord James Hope with whom she travelled to St.Petersburg in 1777 and had favourable reception from Empress Catherine.

CARR [Кар]. Anglicised version of Kerr. Capt. ROBERT C. 1610 commanded a company of mercenary cavalry at Klushino where despite his bravery Russians were beaten by Poles.

JOHN C. 1615 came to Moscow with his uncle J.Shaw and others, began to serve the Tsar and got married, but died shortly and was succeeded by his brother THOMAS [Фома Иванович],"a foreigner of Scottish land", founder of Russian noble family of Kar. 1618 the youngest brother, ROBERT, joined him with recommendation to the Tsar from King James, went back soon, but reappeared in 1628 and probably fought in Smolensk War.

Thomas was granted an estate near Nizhny Novgorod in 1625. His sons GABRIEL, Moscow nobleman in 1658, and PHILIP converted to Orthodoxy with their families. All of their male descendants were soldiers, of whom most famous was

VASILY ALEXEYEVICH KAR (1730-1806). He took part in Seven Years' War and the coup that put Catherine II on the throne, won a star of St.Stanislaus in Poland and became major-gen. and commander of Foreign Legion against the Turks. He suffered disgrace having failed to suppress the Pugachev rising in 1773 and set about to improve his estate near Kaluga making it one of the richest and best-managed in the region by the time Emperor Paul pardoned him.

The family survived into 20th century, and there were many others Carrs, Kerrs and Kers in Russia. {RGADA, f.150, op.1, 1615, No.2; RGIA, f.1343, op.23, Nos.1858, 2047; RBC}.

1632 A.Leslie's regt. included at least four "Kars".

JOHN C. Traveller whose tour in 1804 included Russia. Published "A Northern Summer, or Travels round the Baltic", L., 1805.

CARRICK [Каррик], WILLIAM. 1783 timber merchant in Russian capital. His son and heir ANDREW (1802-1860, St.Petersburg) married Jessie Lauder in Edinburgh 1827. Their sons were

WILLIAM (1827, Edinburgh-1878, St.Petersburg). Pioneer of Russian photography. Graduate of St.Petersburg Academy of Arts. 1859 opened his photo studio in the capital assisted by J.Macgregor. Unlike most colleagues he preferred to portray humble folk and produced famous "Russian Types" series. Made portraits of Russian writers and peasants of Simbirsk region, pictures of I.S.Turgenev's country house, reproduced paintings etc. His brother

GEORGE LYON C. (1840-1908). Studied medicine at Edinburgh, MD St.Andrews. 1865 back in Russia, doctor to British Embassy and many prominent Russians including Princes Volkonsky, M.P. Mussorgsky and Beketov-Bloks. 1877 "The Scotsman"'s correspondent during Russo-Turkish War, awarded order of St.Stanislaus. Wrote on koumiss (fermented mare's milk) and used it at his sanatorium near Orenburg, named Janetovka after his niece. 1884 demonstrated his achievements at International Health Exhibition in London. {F.Ashbee in Caledonian Phalanx, pp.90-105}.

1791 CHRISTOPHER C. married M.Robinson in St.Petersburg and had issue. {RBC}.

CARRUTHERS, JOHN PATRICK. Merchant, from 1830s stayed in St.Petersburg and Odessa where his children were born. 1840s British Vice-Consul at Taganrog. {RBC, III}.

CATHCART [Каткарт], Lord CHARLES (1721-1776). Fought at Fontenoy. 1768-1772 British Ambassador in Russia. His daughter CATHERINE was born in St.Petersburg 1770 (the Empress being godmother) and his wife JANE, nee Hamilton, died there 1771. {RBC, I}. His elder son and heir

Lord WILLIAM SCHAW C. (1755-1843). General. 1812 sent to Russia as British Ambassador. Accompanied Emperor Alexander I on campaigns 1812-4, received Russian orders of St.Andrew and St.George. 1814 created 1st Earl of C. In Russia until 1820. {DNB, III, pp.1194-8}.

CHAMBERS [Чамберс] , JOHN. Scot in Muscovite service, possibly army officer. His son

JOHN [Иван Иванович] (1650, Moscow-1708x). 1678 as ruitmaster wounded at Chigirin. Then one of principal military advisors to young

Tsar Peter and first colonel of Semionovsky Guards which he commanded in Azov expeditions and Great Northern War. 1701 major-gen., took part in first Russian victory over Swedes at Orestfer. 1704 prominent at capture of Narva, made lt.-gen. and knight of St.Andrew. 1708 dismissed after Russian defeat at Golovchin, but a Major CHAMBERS (apparently his son) was wounded at Poltava 1709. {P. Gordon, Diary; Ustrialov}.

CHARYKOV [Чарыков] N.V.   Historian and diplomat. Published "Cosmography of 1670" (St.Petersburg, 1878-81), an early Russian source of information about Scotland. Wrote a profound and detailed work on P.Menzies: "Posol'stvo v Rim i sluzhba v Moskve Pavla Meneziya". St.Petersburg, 1906. 1901 he spent some time in Scotland and archives of Edinburgh and Aberdeen. 1910s Russian agent at the Vatican.

CHERKASOV [Черкасов], Baron ALEXANDER IVANOVICH (1728-1788). Studied in Britain, mostly at Cambridge 1742-7 and 1752-6 along with his brother IVAN (1732-1811). Possibly visited Scotland or even studied medicine at Edinburgh. {Cross, By the Banks, pp.117-8}.

CHRISTIE [Кристи], JOHN. Lived in St.Petersburg from 1790s and died there1806, aged 36. His children were MARY ANNE (1799-1801), JANE (*1801), JOHN (1803-1804) and ROBERT (*1804).
     There were others based in Russian capital including Dr. ALEXANDER C. who died 1842, aged 47. {RBC}.
     Rev. JAMES C. wrote "Men and Things Russian, or Holiday Travels in the Land of the Czar". Edin., 1879.

CLARK, CLERK [Кларк,Клерк].   ALEXANDER C. (+1722, Moscow). Goldsmith from Narva, worked for Russian court and Armory from 1691 {Russkoye zoloto XIV-nachala XX v.Moscow, 1987, p.230}.
     GEORGE C. Engineer at Carron foundry, came to Russia 1786 with C.Gascoigne. His son was
     Engineer-Gen. MATTHEW [Матвей Егорович] C. (1776-1846). Directed state ironworks in St.Petersburg. Involved in major projects as General Staff building, Alexandrinsky Theatre, Narva Gate and Winter Palace. Left a big family. {RBC, Caledonian Phalanx, p.75}.
     CLARKE (?). Described his experience of Russia in his "Travels" {Steuart, p.122-3}.

Sir GEORGE DOUGLAS C. of Penicuik, Bart. 1872 visited Russia {SRO, GD 18/2079}.

CLARK. Scottish industrialist. 1895 had an audience with Emperor Nicholas II in St.Petersburg, probably about construction of Trans-Siberian railway {Dnevniki Nikolaya II, p.57}.

CLAYHILLS [Клейгельс,Клайгильс]. Came from Invergowrie, Angus. Moved to Riga in 17th century, Russian subjects from 1710 {P. Gordon, Diary}.

Gen. NIKOLAY VASILYEVICH KLEYGILS was Prefect of Warsaw Police from 1888, then Governor-Gen. of Volyn, Podolia and Kiev. Adopted coat of arms similar to that of his Scottish namesakes{Steuart, p.55; RGIA, f.1343, op.23, Nos.3619-20}.

CLELAND [Клеланд]. Lieutenant. 1764 joined Russian Navy with C.Douglas, S.Greig and others. Volunteer in Admiral Poliansky's squadron, but left Russian service in a year. {OMS.IV, p.87}.

COATS [Котс]. Heir of Thomas C. (1809-1883), textile magnate from Paisley. 1890 came to St.Petersburg with his partners Brook, Clark and "Hirss" and made a deal with Russian Secretary of State A.A.Polovtsov setting up a joint thread manufacture with capital of 12 mln roubles. {Polovtsov. Dnevnik, II, Moscow, 1966}.

COBLEY [Кобле], THOMAS [Фома Александрович] (1761-1828). Orphaned and brought up at Leghorn with his sister HENRIETTA (1764-1843) and followed her to Russia when she married Capt. N.S. Mordvinov in 1783. They are usually considered English, but A.O.Smirnova-Rosset, who knew Thomas well, invariably calls him a Scot adding that he was fond of "our Scottish songs and tales of the dead". He rose to major-gen. and Commandant of Odessa where he held an estate known as Koblevka, married a Cossack girl and left a son, APOLLON, and a daughter, CLAUDIA. {A.O.Smirnova-Rosset. Dnevnik, Vospominaniya. M., 1989}.

COCHRANE [Кокрен], JOHN. 1784 came to St.Petersburg, aged 34, as master stonemason to work under C.Cameron. 1786 employed with A.Menelaws in construction of St.Joseph's Cathedral in Mogilev {SSR, No.10, 1988, pp.63,71}.

JOHN DUNDAS C. (1780-1825). Capt. of British Navy and pedestrian traveller. 1820-2 walked across Russia from St.Petersburg to Okhotsk on the Pacific coast in 16 months. Lived in Kamchatka where he married a daughter of local official and took her back to Britain 1823. Suspected by some Russians as a spy. His "Narrative of a Pedestrian Journey through Russia and Siberian Tartary", L., 1824, had great success. Died on another expedition in South America.

WILLIAM (+1859, aged 64) and MARY C. (1794-1879) buried at Smolensky cemetery, St.Petersburg.

COLLEY, COLLIE [Колли]. Capt. ARCHIBALD COLLIE served with A.Leslie's regt. in Moscow 1632 and probably besieged Smolensk. {RGADA, f.210, op.1, No.78}.

WILLIAM COLLEY (ca.1740-1789x). Came from Gourock, worked as blacksmith in St.Petersburg. 1766 married Louisa Schubin. Of his grandsons HENRY [Андрей Яковлевич] (1795-1859) was "1st Guild" merchant, director of the Moscow office of State Commercial Bank and hereditary honorary citizen, and CHARLES [Карл Яковлевич] (1809-1859) won a star of St.Stanislaus, 3rd class, as surgeon with the Guards, which entitled him to hereditary nobility.

The family produced several scholars of distinction and the architect NIKOLAY C. (1894-1966). {RBC; RGIA, f.1343, op.23, No.5355 & op.39, No.2220; information from A.V.Gromov-Colley}.

COLQUHOUN, ROBERT. 1843 married Maria Ghidella in St.Petersburg. {RBC, III}.

COLVILLE. British general. Of the Viscounts of Culross family. Fought in Crimean War. Visited Russia in Alexander II's reign and received order of St.Stanislaus. {Diary in family archive}.

COLYAR [Кольер], AUGUSTINE. Tutor to V.P.Davydov. Apparently advised his ward to go to Edinburgh University and stayed with him in Scotland 1825-8. Revisited Edinburgh, Selkirk and Abbotsford later. 1840 married Anne Park in St.Petersburg. {M.P.Alexeyev. Russko-angliyskiye literaturnyye sviazi.M., 1982}.

CONSTANTINE [Константин Николаевич], Grand Duke (1827, St.Petersburg-1892, Pavlovsk). 2nd son of Emperor Nicholas I. Served in Navy from midshipman to Gen.-Admiral, one of his instructors was Capt.Moffat. 1847 arrived in London, met R.Murchison and made a long trip to Scotland in the company of F.P.Luttke, F.I.Brunnow and others. His route by land and water lay through Beattock, Glasgow, Trossachs, Dumbarton, Inveraray, Oban, Iona, Glencoe, Taymouth, Perth (he became Freeman of the burgh), Edinburgh and Melrose. Spent several days hunting at Blair Atholl. {TsGAVMF, f.224, op.1, Nos.5-7}.

COOK [Кук], JOHN (1712, Hamilton-1790, ibid.). Doctor. 1736 got a job in St.Petersburg naval hospital. 1740 moved to Astrakhan with his patron Prince M.Golitsyn and joined him on a mission to Persia. Later chief surgeon at Riga. 1751 returned to Scotland with his wife and three children. Widely interested in natural history and wrote "Voyages and Travels through the Russian Empire, Tartary and Part of the Kingdom of Persia", Edin., 1770.
ALEXANDER C. Uncle to explorer Capt.James C. Ran a rope-walk in Kronshtadt. His daughter SARAH (1752-1793) married S.Greig in 1768. {RBC, I}.

COOPER [Купер], DAVID. 1632 "sub-ruitmaster" in A.Leslie's company and regt.
Lt.-Col. COOPER enlisted in Russian army 1661. Infantry Col. JOHN C. (same?) 1678 took part in Chigirin campaign along with Lt.-Col. THOMAS C., who was requested by D.W.Graham for his regt. in 1683. "Cooper's regt." fought in Great Northern War. {Gordon, Diary; RGADA, f.150, op.1, 1661, No.28; Ustrialov}.

CORMICK, JOHN. Mid-1820s visited Russia. 1826 wrote a letter to Sir John MacNeill about the Decembrist rising in St.Petersburg {SRO, GD 371/25/9}.

CORRAN, also Cock or Cocker, DAVID. (+x1529). Scot in Danish service from 1496. Denmark King of Arms. Danish envoy to Muscovy 1506, 1507 (with four Scottish cannon founders sent to Grand Duke Vasily III by his ally King Johan of Denmark, uncle to James IV,

King of Scots), 1513, 1514, 1519 and 1527. Also headed missions from Copenhagen to Scotland (1517,1518,1525). Often confused with fellow Scot P.Davidson. {T.Riis. Should Auld Acquaintance Be Forgot... Odense, 1988}.

COWIE, THOMAS. Died in St.Petersburg 6/6/1780, aged 23 {RBC, I}.

CRANSTON [Кринстон], JOHN. Scots officer in 17th-century Muscovy. {RIB, XXVIII}.

CRAWFORD [Кроуфорд,Крафорт,Краперт], ALEXANDER (+1651x). Colonel. 1629 came to serve Russia after career in Denmark and Sweden. 1632-4 fought at Smolensk. 1639 taught Western tactics to the Streltsy. 1646 petitioned to take his brother JOHN into Tsar's employ. Engaged in producing potash and invited dyers from abroad. {Stashevsky, Smolenskaya voyna; Soloviev,V}. His daughter married

THOMAS (+1685), son of Hugh C. of Jordanhill and colonel in Russia, whose younger brother was

DANIEL C. (+1674, Moscow). In Russia as infantry colonel from 1650s. 1660 taken prisoner by Poles at Chudnov. 1661 back in Moscow with P.Gordon and P.Menzies who joined his regt. Major-gen. by 1669. His son

Major DANIEL C. (+1691) married Mary, daughter of Patrick Gordon, and had a posthumous son, DANIEL {P.Gordon, Diary}.

"Podrotnik" ALEXANDER, Sergeant HENRY, Corporal HUGH and Private THOMAS C. were in A.Leslie's regt. in 1632. {RGADA, f.210, op.1, No.78}.

HUGH C. 1660s colonel.

LAWRENCE C. 1674 asked permission to go from Russia "to his fatherland".

Lt.-Col. THOMAS C. served in 1690s.

THOMAS C. (+1787). 1784 in Russia as C.Cameron's plasterer, aged 27. {SSR. No.10, 1988; RBC}.

CRICHTON [Крейтон], Capt. 1610 commanded a cavalry company at Klushino {Steuart, p.27}.

JOHN C. Army officer, 17th century {RIB, XXVIII}.

Dr. ALEXANDER C. (1763, Edinburgh-1856, Kent). 1804 became physician-in-ordinary to Emperor Alexander I. Directed Russia's Civil Medical Department. Expert in chemistry, botany and geology. Discovered method to refine vegetable oil with sulphuric acid. Wrote "Pharmacopoeia in usum nosocomii pauperum Petropolitani" etc. 1820 returned to Britain and was knighted {Caledonian Phalanx, pp.59-60). His children were born in St.Petersburg and his nephew was

Sir ARCHIBALD WILLIAM [Василий Петрович] C. (1791-1865). Actual State Councillor and doctor to Russian Court. Studied at Edinburgh, took part in French wars. 1816 accompanied Grand Duke Nicholas (future Emperor) to Scotland. Wrote on cholera etc. He founded the Russian noble family of C. {RGIA, f.1343, op.23, Nos.8742-3; RBC}.

Another Russian branch, called "KREYTAN", is obviously also of Scots origin {RGIA, f.1343, op.36, No.12755}.

CROMBIE, ALEXANDER. Married 1) Joan Kerr, 1826 and 2) Margaret Sclanders, 1845, in St.Petersburg {RBC}.

CROWN [Кроун,Крон], ROBERT [Роман Васильевич] (1753, Scotland-1841, St.Petersburg). 1788 joined Russian Navy as lieutenant. 1824 admiral. Had issue including
ALEXANDER MALCOLM C. (1823-1900), vice-admiral. {RGIA, f.1343, op.23, No.9316 & op.36, No.12925; RBC; OMS}.

CUMMING [Кумминг]. Officer in command of 5 battallions of Russian Hussars during Russo-Swedish War of 1741-3 under J.Keith. 1757 Major-Gen. "Coming" (same?) was in charge of General Hospital in Moscow {RNL, Avt.136, No.49; Soloviev, XII, p.415}.
ALEXANDER C. lived in St.Petersburg 1800-10s {RBC}.

CUNNINGHAM [Кунингам], ROBERT. 1613 left Polish service for that of Russia with other Scots of the Bely garrison. 1624 King James asked the Tsar to release him, but he fought at Smolensk 1632-4 {RIB, XXVIII; Stashevsky, Smolenskaya voyna}.
Ensign NINIAN C. present at muster of A.Leslie's regt.1632. His pay was 10 roubles a month.

Col. WILLIAM [Василий] C. served in 1660s-70s {RGADA, f.141, op.3, 1663, No.172 & f.150, op.1, 1679,No.7}. His sons must have been Ensigns IVAN and PIOTR who went on Chigirin campaign 1678.

Major PAVEL C. and Capt. NIKITA C. 1698 served in Semionovsky Guards under J.Chambers. NIKITA VASILYEVICH (1675-1736), brigadier, and his son SERGEY (1715-1750),sub-lieutenant, are buried in the Church of the Resurrection "in Barashi", Moscow.

THOMAS C. 1738 lieutenant. Served at Archangel and Kronshtadt. 1745 resigned. {OMS, II}.

DAVID C. (1758-1807). 1784 in Russia as C.Cameron's stonemason and assistant, worked at Tsarskoye Selo, Peterhof and St.Petersburg {SSR, No.10, 1988, pp.63-5}.

DALGLEISH, ALEXANDER. 1828 married Mary Hague in St.Petersburg and had issue. {RBC}.

DALKEITH, Lord CHARLES MONTAGUE DOUGLAS SCOTT (1772-1819). Eldest son of 3rd Duke of Buccleuch, then 4th Duke. 1793 visited Russia. 1814 D.P.Severin met him in Scotland and remarked: "I count the Duke of Buccleuch and his family among my most pleasant acquaintances. His country house is seven miles from Edinburgh where he lives with amazing luxury as befits a lord. The Duke was in Russia 20 years ago and likes Russians". {Alexeyev, pp.267, 345, 377}.

DALRYMPLE, J. 2nd husband of Anne, Countess of Haddington, eldest daughter of C.Gascoigne. 1803 he attended wedding of her sister Elizabeth Gascoigne and G.A.Pollen in St.Petersburg. {RBC, I, f.141v.}.

DALYELL [Далиел], THOMAS (1615, Binns,West Lothian-1685,Edinburgh). Royalist general, captured at Worcester but escaped from London Tower. 1656 taken into Russian service with W.Drummond and W.Johnston on recommendation of King Charles II. Commanded a regt. during Russo-Polish wars, got rank of full general and estates near Polotsk and Smolensk where he succeeded A.Leslie as Governor. 1665 allowed to return home on request of King Charles to become commander of King's army in Scotland. He suppressed Covenanters who called him "bluidie Muscovite" and "Muscovy beast". 1681 raised Royal Scots Greys. Some of the things he used in Russia are preserved at the Binns. His eldest son

THOMAS served under his father as captain in Smolensk staying behind for some time after his departure. 1685 created baronet. {RGADA, fonds 27, 141, 145, 150, 233, 396; P.Gordon, Diary; The Binns Papers. Edin., 1936}.

DASHKOVA [Дашкова], Princess YEKATERINA ROMA-NOVNA (1743, St.Petersburg-1810, Moscow). Sister of Russian Ambassadors to Britain, Counts Alexander and Semion Vorontsov. 1776 with her children ANASTASIA (1760-1831) and PAVEL (1763-1807) arrived in Edinburgh and settled in the Palace of Holyroodhouse. They spent over 2,5 years in Scottish capital and often met Adam Smith,

W.Robertson, H.Blair, A.Ferguson and other eminent scholars. 1777 they went on a Higland tour through Stirling, Perth, Dunkeld, Taymouth, Inveraray, Loch Lomond and Dumbarton. Dashkova's journal (unpublished) is the first Russian account of those parts. In gratitude for "the most peaceful and happy period" of her life she presented the University with a rare collection of Russian medals. She later directed both Russian Academy and St.Petersburg Academy of Sciences ensuring honorary membership for W.Robertson and J.Black.

Prince PAVEL [Павел Михайлович] D. studied at Edinburgh University under his mother's guidance, wrote "Dissertatio philosophica inauguralis de Tragoedia"; M.A. 1779. Made Freeman of Edinburgh and Dumbarton. Later lt.-gen. and Marshal of Moscow Nobility. {Princess E.R.Dashkova. Zapiski. Leningrad, 1985; Cross, By the Banks, pp.131-6, 237-8}.

DAVIDSON [Давидсон], PETER (ca.1450, Aberdeen-1520, Copenhagen). "Peder Skotte" or "Petrus Davidis de Scotia Aberdonensis" in Danish sources. First Scot and Danish Ambassador in Russia known by name. Studied and taught at Cologne. 1479 one of founders of Copenhagen University, then its vice-chancellor. 1495 sent to Muscovy by King Johan (uncle to James IV, King of Scots) to confirm the Russo-Danish alliance of 1493 with "conclusive letters". Often confused with another Scot in Danish employ, D.Corran. {T.Riis. Should Auld Acquaintance Be Forgot. Odense, 1988}.

WILLIAM and GILBERT D. were in A.Leslie's regt. in Moscow 1632.

DAVIDSONS. From mid-17th century noblemen of Poland, then of Vilno region of Russian Empire. Had a stag or in their coat of arms, like their Scottish clansmen. Claimed comital title, but failed to prove it. {RGIA, f.1343, op.20, No.34b}.

DAVIDSON. Manager of Emperor Alexander I's farm near St.Petersburg. 1802 went to Britain to hire workers, buy stock, seeds and implements. EMILY D. (+1804, St.Petersburg) probably his daughter {Cross, By the Banks, p.89; RBC}.

DAVIE [Деви], ALEXANDER (1761-1827, St.Petersburg). 1784 in Russia as C.Cameron's smith. Worked at Olonets foundries. Had issue including

CHRISTOPHER (1801-1853x). Lt.-colonel of engineers, director of Zlatoust factory. 1853 he and family acknowledged as noblemen of Kazan region. {RGIA, f.1343, op.20, No.727; RBC}.

DAVYDOV [Давыдов], later Count ORLOV-DAVYDOV, VLADIMIR PETROVICH (1809-1882). 1825 came to Scotland with his tutor A.Colyar. 1826-8 studied at Edinburgh University. Often visited Sir Walter Scott whom he informed about Russian affairs. He declared, "My affection for Scotland in which I have passed so many happy days, is second to no other attachment within my breast". Kept in touch with his Scottish friends and was frequently mistaken for a Scot because of his accent and manners. Served with Russian Foreign Ministry and inherited his grandfather's title and fortune. {Alexeyev}.

DEMIDOV [Демидов], PAVEL GRIGORYEVICH (1738-1821). Came from ennobled family of Ural industrialists. Studied in Britain in early 1760s. Ca. 1760 made Freeman of Glasgow; visited Carron works. 1803 founded Demidov Lyceum in Yaroslavl. {RGADA, f.1267; Cross, By the Banks}.

DENBIGH [Демби], GEORGE (1841-1894x). 1870s settled in Vladivostok, then moved to Sakhalin and became Russian subject. He and his three sons engaged in fur trade, hunting, fishing and food processing. Chekhov describes him as Scottish in his "Island of Sakhalin". 1894 D. was visited by a Mr.Graham-Campbell. {P.Barlow, "Chekhov's Far Eastern Scotsman", SSR, No.8, 1987, pp.7-15}.

DENNISON [Денисон], FRANCIS (ca.1750-1790). 1771 joined Russian Navy as midshipman and rose to capt. "of brigadier's rank". 1788 commanded a ship at Hogland against the Swedes. Died of wounds after battle of Viborg. Married Ruth Farquharson in St.Petersburg; their son ARCHIBALD ROSS died in infancy. {OMS, III; RBC, I}.

DERIABIN [Дерябин], ANDREY FEDOROVICH (1770-1820). Son of a Siberian priest. Studied at Mining Corps in St.Petersburg which he later directed. 1797 sent to Britain to perfect engineering skills and visited Glasgow and Carron works. Met James Watt. {RBS, "D", pp.327-9; Cross, By the Banks}.

DESNITSKY [Десницкий], SEMION YEFIMOVICH (ca.1740, Nezhin-1789, Moscow). Entered Moscow University. 1761 sent to Glasgow with I.A.Tretyakov and studied under Adam Smith and James Millar. 1767 Doctor of Law; returned to Moscow to become first professor of law there lecturing in Latin,Russian and English. 1783 member of Russian Academy. Called "Father of Russian jurisprudence", but also interested in literature and agriculture. {RBS; Cross, By the Banks, pp.122-8}.

DEWAR, MORIS. 1784, aged 25, came to St.Petersburg as C.Cameron's stonemason, but dismissed for negligence 1786. {SSR, No.10, 1988, p.59}. 1787 DIANA "DOOAR", possibly a relative of his, married John MacLaren in St.Petersburg.

DICK [Дик], ANDREW. (1750, Scotland-1794, St.Petersburg). Master stonemason, worked under C.Cameron in Russia from 1784. Opened his own workshop in the capital. His daughter (?) MARGARET D. +1799, aged 19.
JOHN D. married Jane Frazer in St.Petersburg, 1803. {SSR, No.10, 1988; RBC}.

DIXON [Диксон]. "Sub-ruitmaster" SIM and drummer HARIE D. served in A.Leslie's regt. 1632.
Lt.-Col. DIXON of Russian army is mentioned by P.Gordon in 1660s, and others appear in 19th-century St.Petersburg. {RBC}.

DOIG, ROBERT (+1817, St.Petersburg,aged 17). Native of Arbroath, served on ship "Alert". {RBC, II}.

DOUGLAS [Дуглас], FRANCIS. Ensign. 1634 on his leave of Tsar's service A.Leslie gave him testimonials in German and Russian. He could be the Capt. Francis D. who turned up in Moscow ca.1650 with a passport from "English Major-Gen. Robert Stirling". {RGADA, f.150, op.1, 1634, No.4 & 1649, No.13}.
Empress Catherine I, consort of Peter the Great, ordered to find her kinsmen the "Duklas" in Kurland. Her aunt married a LAURIN D. and had six sons of whom SIMON D. lived in Kreuzburg in 1710s after Russia conquered Livonia. {Soloviev, IX, p.627}.

Counts WILHELM (1683-1763) and GUSTAV-OTTO (1687-1763x) D. Swedish officers of the Scottish D.-Whittinghame line. Captured by Russians at Poltava 1709. The elder was released and went back to Sweden 1722, the younger chose to serve Peter the Great becoming first Russian Governor of Finland 1717, and then of Reval 1737-40. His turbulent career featured imprisonment for murder of a Russian captain, cruelties in war against the Turks and a treason charge, but he was still thought of as "an able general and good administrator". 1751 he retired after whipping a Livonian nobleman to death. His son was page at Russian court, but the line died out soon. {RGVIA, f.160; Steuart, pp.87-9}.

Chevalier WILLIAM MACKENZIE D., Scots Jacobite, came to Russia with secret missions on behalf of French Court 1755 and 1756-7. {Soloviev, XII}.

CHARLES D. 1764 joined Russian Navy with S.Greig and others as rear-admiral in Poliansky squadron, but resigned the following year to become rear-admiral in Britain. {OMS, III}.

JAMES D. 1784 arrived in Russia, aged 26, as one of C.Cameron's stonemasons. {SSR, No.10, 1988}.

Lady YEVDOKIA D.-HAMILTON, nee Sukhanova-Podkolzina (1846-1887) was buried in Moscow.

GEORGE NORMAN D. (1868-1952). Born Germany of Scots parents. Spent childhood at Tilquhillie castle near Banchory, then lived mostly abroad. On diplomatic service in St.Petersburg 1894-6. Took up science and literature. Wrote "Unprofessional Tales", "South Wind" and "Looking Back", his memoirs.

DOWNIE, JAMES. 1821 married Charlotte Edwards in St.Petersburg and had sons JAMES (*1822) and FREDERICK (*1823) {RBC, II}.

DRUMMOND [Друмонд,Дромант], GEORGE. 1615 officer who came via Archangel to Moscow to seek employment.

WILLIAM D. (ca.1617-1688). 4th Lord Madderty, sometimes styled "of Cromlix". Fought against Cromwell, fled to continent. 1656 went to Moscow as major-gen. with T.Dalyell on recommendation of King Charles II. 1662 defeated Poles near Chausy, shortly promoted to lt.-gen. and commander of Smolensk garrison and granted an estate. 1665 allowed to leave Russia on request of his King. 1686 created Viscount of Strathallan. Buried in Dunblane Cathedral.

MIKITA DAVYDOVICH D. served in 1670s as colonel of Belgorod regt. receiving 40 roubles a month. {RGADA, fonds 27, 150, 396; P.Gordon, Diary}.

Capt.-Lt. "DRUMANT" of the Guards was a signer of the accusation against Tsarevich Alexey, son of Peter the Great, in 1718.

DUFF [Дуфф], JAMES. Officer in Muscovite army, 17th century. {RIB, XXVIII}.

DUFFUS [Дуффус], KENNETH SUTHERLAND, 3rd Lord (+1732, Kronshtadt). Capt. in Scottish Navy and Jacobite. After 1715 forfeited and fled to Sweden. 1722 taken into Russian Navy as rear-admiral, superintendent of St.Petersburg dockyard and member of Admiralty College. Commanded ports of Reval and Kronshtadt. 1726 demoted for flogging an Estonian nobleman, but soon pardoned. Married daughter of Swedish admiral Sjoblad and had a son who claimed his title. {OMS, I, pp.142-4}. Cf. Sutherland.

DUGDALE [Дугдаль], ROBERT (ca.1745-1790x). 1769 enlisted in Russian Navy as lieutenant. 1770 capt.-lt., bravely commanded a fire-ship against the Turks at Chesme. Won order of St.George, 4th class and promoted to rear-admiral. Served in Baltic and Black Sea fleets until 1790. {OMS, III, pp.510-1}.

DUGUID. SARAH "DOUGOUD" died 21/1/1813 in St. Petersburg, aged 30. {RBC, II}.

DUNBAR [Дунбар], ROBERT. 1600 accepted for military service in Muscovy along with D.Gilbert. Apparently served with the bodyguard of Tsar Boris Godunov and was involved in events of "Time of Troubles". {Steuart, p.25}.

DUNCAN [Дункан]. JAMES D. ("YAKOV DUMKOV") from Bervie came to Russia 1630 to serve in Tsar's army and probably fought at Smolensk 1632-4. {Stashevsky, Smolenskaya voyna}.

ANDREW D. 1801 married Sarah Stranack in St.Petersburg.

JAMES D. Engineer. 1802 came to St.Petersburg to modernise the Mint there. 1804 married Martha Twycross and had issue. {RBC}.

JAMES [Яков Васильевич] D. (*1837). Pledged allegiance to Russia. Telegraphist in Winter Palace and Tsarskoye Selo, then secretary and treasurer to Grand Duke Vladimir, Aulic Councillor and knight of St.Vladimir,4th class. 1890 granted hereditary noble status. Married Elizabeth Isherwood and fathered ELIZABETH (1869-1906), JAMES (*1872) and PAUL (*1879). {RGIA, f.1343, op.20, No.3763}.

DUNCANSON [Дункансон], DAVID (1770, Airth, Stirlingshire-1844, Moscow). 1803 married Janet Gray in St.Petersburg. Their daughter JESSIE (1811-1881) married James Hercules Scott.{RBC, I}.

EDEN, ROBERT (1804-1886,Inverness). Englishman by birth. 1851 consecrated Bishop of Moray and Ross. 1862 elected Primus of Scottish Episcopal Church. 1866 went on a spiritual mission to Russia, supported rapprochement between his Church and Orthodoxy and wrote "Impressions of a Recent Visit to Russia on Intercommunion with the Eastern Orthodox Church". Emperor Alexander II presented five Russian icons to him; they are preserved in St.Andrew's Cathedral, Inverness {DNB, VI, pp.360-1}.

EDWARDS [Эдвардс], DAVID. Scots officer in Muscovite army, 17th century {RIB, XXVIII}.

EDWARDS. Scottish family said to have settled in Russia in 18th century. They had a house in Ozerki near St.Petersburg. A girl of the family (*ca.1870) married Mikhail Zubakin, an army officer. Their son was the writer Boris Zubakin (1894-1937). {Novy Mir, No.7, 1992, p.91}.

EL(L)IOT [Эл(л)иот], THOMAS. Lived in St.Petersburg 1760s. His daughter ELIZABETH baptized there 1770.

HENRY [Андрей Иванович] E. (ca.1760-1822). 1783 lieutenant of Russian Navy. 1788 capt.-lt., fought in Russo-Swedish war. 1798-1800 commanded a frigate in Russo-British campaign against France. 1809 rear-admiral. Retired by 1811. Most of his descendants served in the army. One of his three sons

JOHN [Иван Андреевич] (1802-1888), major-gen., was proud of his connection with Eliots of Minto and Redheugh and members of his family still spoke with a Scots accent in 20th century. {RGIA, f.1343, op.21, No.584; RBC; OMS, V, pp.398-9}.

Sir GILBERT E., apparently 1st Earl of Minto (1751-1814), visited Russia ca.1780 and met Admiral S.Greig.

ELLIS [Эллис]. This family, settled in Russia in late 18th century, had Scottish connections and was related to Mounseys. Gen. ALEXANDER E. (1825-1907) was Commandant of SS.Peter and Paul Fortress, St.Petersburg. {Y.Epatko, "The Ellis family in Russia", SSR, No.10, 1988, pp.239-49}.

ELPHINSTONE [Элфинстон], GABRIEL (2nd half of 16th century). "Valiant Scottish captaine" who served in Denmark and Sweden, took part in expedition in search of North-East passage to China, was captured in Siberia by Tartars and escaped to Moscow, which must have been about 1581-5. He joined Tsar's army and is probably identical with the Scot Gabriel (+ca.1605), capt. of the guard and physician to Tsar Boris Godunov. {Steuart, p.19; RBS}.

THOMAS "ERBENSTRAM", a "nobleman's son" from Dumfries, became officer in Russian army 1630 and probably took part in Smolensk war. {Stashevsky, Smolenskaya voyna}.

JOHN E. (1722-1785). 1769 became rear-admiral in Russian Navy. Commanded a squadron against the Turks and fought at Chesme 1770. After disagreement over plans of campaign and the loss of his flagship he was recalled to St.Petersburg and returned to Britain in 1771 with his sons, midshipmen JOHN and SAMUEL WILLIAM. But the latter rejoined Russian Navy 1783 as capt. of 2nd rank, won the order of St.George,4th class, fighting the Swedes and died of wounds 1790. Their younger brother ROBERT enlisted in Russian Navy as lieutenant 1786, fought in Swedish war 1788-90 and in campaign against France 1798-1800. He rose to capt. of 1st rank and retired as State Councillor 1808. {OMS, V, pp. 399-402; Steuart, pp.126-8}.

JOHN, son of Capt.ALEXANDER FRANCIS E. of British Navy, was baptized in St.Petersburg 1824.

ERSKINE [Арескин], ROBERT (1677, Alva-1718, Olonets). Son of Sir Charles E. of Alva and kinsman of Earl of Mar. Studied medicine in Edinburgh, Paris and Utrecht. 1704 in Russia as doctor to Prince Menshikov but soon became chief physician to Tsar Peter and State Councillor. As President of Apothecaries' (later Medical) Chancery he reformed both civil and military medicine in the country. He supervised hospitals and pharmacies, founded a botanic garden in St.Petersburg, collected Russia's earliest herbal, discovered spring waters for medical treatment, planned scientific expeditions to Caucasus and Siberia and was in charge of Peter's natural history museum, the Kunstkammer, and his library. A Jacobite, he invited many Scots to serve the Tsar. {Academy of Sciences Archive, St.Petersburg; Caledonian Phalanx, pp.47-9}.

FAMINTSYN [Фаминцын]. This name stems from Christopher Tobias Thomson, a Scot in Poland. By 1681 his great-grandson IVAN moved to Russia and was ennobled. His son YEGOR (+1731) was major-gen. and Commandant of St.Petersburg fortress. Other noted members of the family were the botanist ANDREY SERGEYEVICH F. (1835-1918) and his brother ALEXANDER (1841-1896), composer and critic. {RGIA, f.1343, op.31, Nos.97-9}.

FARQUHARSON [Фарварсон], Henry [Андрей Данилович] (ca.1675,Aberdeenshire?-1739, St.Petersburg). Graduate and lecturer of Marischal College, Aberdeen. 1698 engaged for Russian service by Tsar Peter in London and directed Russia's first secular educational institution, the Moscow School of Mathematics and Navigation, later the Naval Academy in St.Petersburg, for nearly 40 years. Published earliest Russian works on mathematics and astronomy ("Tables of Logarithms", "Euclid's Elements" etc.) and helped to introduce Arabic numerals for Cyrillic. An expert cartographer and surveyor he laid out a new road between Moscow and St.Petersburg. Achieved rank of brigadier. {D.Fedosov, "Henry Farquharson: A Scottish mathematician in Russia" in: Aberdeen and Europe: The First Three Centuries. Aberdeen, 1995}.

JOHN F. (1730-1807, St.Petersburg) 1750s settled in Russian capital. One of his daughters, RUTH (*1761), married Capt.F.Dennison in 1785. {RBC, I}.

FEILD, ANDREW FORBES. 1815 married Sarah Holliday in St.Petersburg and had issue. {RBC}.

FERGUS(S)ON. ROBERT "FARGASON" 1783 entered Russian service as midshipman. 1784 promoted to lieutenant and sent to Archangel where he died. {OMS, V, p.257}.

The name appears in Poland from 17th century. Peter F. was adopted by his uncle, the rich merchant Peter Tepper, and rose to noble status ca.1789. His son WILHELM TEPPER de FERGUSON (ca.1775-1823x) settled in Russia. After a spell in the army he became music teacher at Tsarskoye Selo Lyceum in 1816 and was very popular with students including the poet Alexander Pushkin. {A.F.Steuart. Papers Relating to Scots in Poland. Edin., 1915, p.223}.

WALTER F. Lived in St.Petersburg with his family around 1831-3. {RBC, III}.

FERMOR [Фермор], GEORGE. Sergeant who came from Sweden to serve the Tsar 1661. {RGADA, f.150, op.1, 1661, No.3}. Possibly fell at siege of Azov 1696. His son (?) was

WILLIAM [Виллим Юрьевич] F. Scots gentleman in Russian army from 1708 as lt.-col. Commanded small garrison of Veprik in Ukraine taken by Swedes with great losses in 1709. Later major-gen. His sons:

WILLIAM [Dbkkbv Dbkkbvjdbx] (1702-1771) active in Danzig campaign 1734, in wars against Turkey 1735-9 and Sweden 1741. 1742 appointed head of Building Chancery and supervised construction in St.Petersburg (Winter Palace etc.) and elsewhere. 1755 full general. During Seven Years' War rejoined the army. Conquered Memel and Konigsberg, became Governor-Gen. of Eastern Prussia and Commander-in-Chief of Russian forces. 1758 Count of Holy Roman Empire, title recognized in Russia. Later senator and Governor of Smolensk. His brother JOHN (*1710) was a brigadier. They married daughters of Lt.-Gen. Robert Bruce, Dorothy Elizabeth and Mary. {RGIA, f.1343, op.31, Nos.687-8 & op.46, Nos.1530-5}.

William's title passed through his daughter to Count Stenbock 1825 while the untitled line was continued by John's descendants. One of them, NIKOLAY F. figures in N.S.Leskov's story "Penniless Engineers".

FERSEN [Ферзен], Counts of Sweden and Russian Empire Claimed descent from a Macpherson who settled in Sweden in 16th century. Fersen is indeed a form of that clan name, and JAMES F. appears in A.Leslie's regt. 1632. {RGIA, f.1343, op.46, Nos.1637-8}.

FINLAYSON, JAMES (ca.1775-1838x). By 1817 employed at state iron works near St.Petersburg. 1820 moved to Tammerfors,Finland, and started his own cotton mill which he ran until 1838. {R.C.Scott. Quakers in Russia. London, 1964, pp.79-80}.

FLECK [Флек]. Ensign ROBERT and Sergeant ALEXANDER F. served in Muscovy under A.Leslie 1632. The former was paid 10 roubles a month. {RGADA, f.210, op.1, No.78}.

FLETCHER, ALEXANDER. Died St.Petersburg, 1822, aged 2 years 2 months.

ROBERT F. 1823 married Hannah Cook in St.Petersburg and died there 1827, aged 58 {RBC ,II}.

FORBES [Форбс], JAMES. Captain under A.Leslie. 28/3/1633 obtained warrant from King and Privy Council of Scotland to recruit 200 Scots for Muscovite service. Took part in Smolensk war. {SRO, PC 11/5A, No.18}.

GEORGE [Юрий Вилимов] "FROBOS" (+1704x). 1675-1700 court goldsmith in Moscow. {Russkoye zoloto XIV-nachala XX v.Moscow, 1987, p.234}.

Lord GEORGE F. (1685-1765). Grandson of Scots laird who settled in Ireland. 1733-4 British Minister in St.Petersburg. Concluded Russo-British commercial treaty. Declined command over Russian Navy offered him by Empress Anne, became Admiral in Royal Navy and Earl of Granard. {DNB, VII}. Another FORBES was British Minister in Russia 1830s.

FORBES. Noblemen of Grand Duchy of Finland, part of Russian Empire. {G.Siven. Suomalainen sukuhakemisto. Helsinki, 1943, p.56}.

ARCHIBALD F. (1838, Moray-1900). 1877-8 correspondent for "Daily News" from the Balkan theatre of Russo-Turkish war. Witnessed main battles of Plevna and Shipka and won Russian order of St.Stanislaus "with swords" for bravery. Met Emperor Alexander II whom he accompanied to St.Petersburg. Wrote "Memories and Studies of War and Peace", L., 1895.

FRANCIS F. (1844-1911). Younger son of London stock-broker. Met Russian Carricks, visited them in St.Petersburg and married Jessie Carrick there in 1868 with his brother EDWARD as best man . Their children were JANET and NEVILL (1883-1929) who often went to Russia. Nevill taught Russian at Oxford and published grammar books, translations of Russian tales etc. {Caledonian Phalanx, pp.94-105}.

FORRAT, or FORRET, ANDREW. Colonel in Russian army. 1662 sent to London with Russian envoy Prince Prozorovsky as his advisor and interpreter. Received testimonials from King Charles II praising his noble lineage and conduct. F. also hired 5 Scots officers for Tsar's service. {PRO 22/60, ff.80-81; P.Gordon, Diary}.

FORRESTER, FRANCIS (1746-1811,St.Petersburg). Partner in firm "Peter & Francis F." of Leith, in St.Petersburg from 1780s. Friend and brother-in-law of C.Cameron whom he helped to hire craftsmen in Scotland. Left a big family. {SSR, No.10, 1988; RBC}.

JAMES F. (1850, Wemyss, Fife-1917x). Ca.1900 moved to Narva where he managed a jute mill. 1917 fled to Britain with his family leaving all their possessions behind.

FORSYTH [Форсайт], DAVID. 1615 arrived in Moscow via Archangel with J.Shaw, J.Carr and other Scots to seek employment. {RGADA, f.150, op.1, 1615, No.2}.

DAVID F. lived in St.Petersburg by 1805 and had issue. {RBC}.

FRANCIS, Rev. ALEXANDER. Congregational minister from Edinburgh. Ca.1891 organized aid for famine-stricken Volga regions in Russia. While there he got gravely ill and prayers for his recovery were said in St.Isaac's Cathedral,St.Petersburg, "first time a non-Russian was thus honoured by Russian Church". He eventually recovered. {Scots Magazine, N.S., XLIII, No.4, 1945, p.254}.

FRASER. Brigadier in Russian army during Great Northern War. 1708 commanded a unit defending St.Petersburg. The Swedes captured a wagon where in his coat notice was found of the approach of strong Russian reinforcements, after which they hastily withdrew. {Sbornik IRIO, L, St.Petersburg, 1886}.

JAMES F. was buried in St.Petersburg 5/1/1750, and many others are later mentioned in RBC.

FRASER. Noble family of Grand Duchy of Finland. Russian subjects from 1809. {Siven, p.57}.

FREER, WILLIAM. 1760s chief surgeon of Russian army. 1768 made a will in Leith. {SRO}.

FULLARTON [Фулертон], ROBERT [Роман], of Dudwick (+1786). Colonel of Russian army in reign of Empress Elizabeth. Fought in Seven Years' War. 1760 major-gen. Died in Scotland, unmarried, but "surrounded by Russian servants". {Semiletniaya voyna. Moscow, 1948; Steuart, p.113, where he is called "John"}.

GABRIEL [Габриель] cf. Elphinstone

GALBRAITH (+x1693). Colonel in Russia from 1680s. Served in Belgorod {P.Gordon, Diary}.

GALLACHER, WILLIAM (1881, Paisley-1965). Communist. Led anti-war campaign of Clyde Workers' Committee. 1920 with John S. Clarke represented Clyde Shop Stewards at 2nd Congress of Communist International in Petrograd and Moscow. Met Lenin. Scored lone goal for English-speaking delegates in their 11-1 demolition by a Moscow football side. Wrote "Revolt on the Clyde", L.,1936, and "The Last Memoirs", L., 1966. M.P. for West Fife.

GALLOWAY [Галловей], HENRY (1765-1828, St.Petersburg). Doctor. 1788-90 took part in Russo-Swedish war. 1801 married Eleonora Barny in St.Petersburg with the poet Derzhavin as best man. 1817 they adopted an infant girl who was christened Eleonora. {RBC}.
Cf. Halloway.

GARDNER [Гарднер], FRANCIS [Франц Яковлевич] (+1790). Timber merchant in Russia from 1746. 1766 set up Russia's first private porcelain manufacture at Verbilki near Dmitrov, Moscow region. It soon acquired fame and produced exquisite "Russian Orders" services for Empress Catherine. Business was carried on by FRANCIS G. II (+1799) and his heirs until 1892; the factory still exists today. Gardners were ennobled, and a lane in Moscow bears their name. {RGIA, f.1343, op.19, Nos.724-5; N.V.Cherny. Farfor Verbilok. Moscow, 1970}.

GARDYNE (?). 1650s Magister ANDREW "GARDINUS", "learned man from Scotland", was pastor of Reformed church in Moscow's "New Foreign Suburb" {Olearius in Rossiya XV-XVII v. glazami inostrantsev, p.413}.

GARFIELD [Гарфильд], ALEXANDER. Of Scottish descent. Directed Bolshoi Theatre in mid 19th century. Married niece of composer A.F.Lvov. Their son was
SERGEY ALEKSANDROVICH GARIN (1873-1927), writer and Bolshevik. {Russkiye pisateli, I}.

GARIOCH [Гариох], GEORGE [Юрий]. Captain. 1647 hired in Holland to serve the Tsar together with J.Stewart and W.Bruce. Despite his unimpressive display of skills at a muster he was not turned down. {Soloviev, V, p.593}.

GARNE [Герн], THOMAS. 1613 surrendered to Russians with other Scots of the Polish garrison at Belaya. 1628 served with "Great regt." in Tula, then evidently took part in Smolensk war and promoted to colonel. He was "in stature taller and greater in his compass of body then any within six kingdomes about him" and was offered to be "King of Bucharia", but refused, having "no stomack to be circumcised". {RGADA, f.150, op.1, 1615, No.2; T.Urquhart. The Jewel. Edin., 1983, p.139}.

GARVINE [Гарвин], THOMAS (1690, Ayr-1766, ibid.?). Studied at Glasgow. By 1713 surgeon in St.Petersburg through protection of R.Erskine. 1715-18 sent on first Russian medical mission to China where he mastered Chinese method of smallpox inoculation. Back in Scotland he became Provost of Ayr. {F.C.Weber.The Present State of Russia. L., 1722-3; R.Burgess, "T.Garvine - Ayrshire surgeon active in Russia", Medical History, XIX, No.1, 1975}.

GASCOIGNE [Гаскойн], CHARLES (1737 or 8-1806, St. Petersburg). Reformer of Russia's industry. Son of army captain and a daughter of Lord Elphinstone. As Director of Carron ironworks he exported cannon (carronades) and sent engineers to Russia, and moved there himself on invitation of S.Greig in 1786, with C.Baird and other specialists. Founded, reorganised and headed factories at Olonets, St.Petersburg, Kronshtadt, Kolpino and Lugansk. Also reconstructed wharfs at Nikolaev, directed Aleksandrovsk textile mill and improved weights and measures. By his first wife he had four daughters, ANNE, MARY, ELIZABETH and MARGARET, and married Anastasia-Jessie Guthrie in 1797. {RNL, f.949, No.17; RBC; Caledonian Phalanx, pp.65-7}.

GEDDES, ISAAC. Lived in Moscow 1630s. 1632 witness to the will of Capt.Wauchope. Probably a merchant or craftsman. {Scottish Soldier Abroad, p.52}.

GAVIN G. (1758-1829) died and buried in St.Petersburg. {RBC, II}.

GEMMILL, JOHN. Paisley merchant who traded in textiles in St.Petersburg and Moscow 1851-4. {SRO, GD 1/504/2-10}.

GIBB(S) [Гиб(с)]. 1632 Corporal HENRY and Private JAMES G. were in A.Leslie's regt. in Moscow. {RGADA, f.210, op.1, No.78}.

GEORGE ALEXANDER and PETER, sons of JOHN G. baptized in St.Petersburg 1806, and others appear later. {RBC}.

GIBSON [Гибсон], ALEXANDER ILYICH. 1650s colonel in command of regt. at Smolensk. Ca. 1656 Colonel JOHN G. came to Russia with his wife and F.Rose and embraced Orthodoxy (rebaptized Alexander?). {RGADA, f.141, op.3, No.23 & f.396, op.1, ch.36, Nos.53201-2; Phipps, p.395}.

MATTHEW G. (1760-1795). 1789 married Mary Wilson in St.Petersburg and died there. {RBC, I}.

SAMUEL G. (+1710) served in Russian Navy from 1704. {OMS, 1}

GIBSONS. Scots family in St.Petersburg and Moscow in 19th and early 20th cent. Directed Moscow branch of Nevsky Stearine Works (Sir William Miller & Co.). {H.Pitcher. The Smiths of Moscow. Cromer, 1984}.

GILBERT [Гилберт], DAVID (+ca.1625). 1600 entered Russian service with R.Dunbar as captain. 1605-6 officer under False Dmitry I, whose guard allegedly included 100 Scots, and False Dmitry II. He then joined the Poles, was imprisoned by Russians for three years and freed through intercession of King James I(VI) in 1617. 1618 G. went back to Muscovy with his son THOMAS and apparently died there. G. was the first Scot to leave an account of his Russian adventures, published in London in 1625. {S.Purchas. His Pilgrimes, III, L., 1625, pp.765-70; Steuart, pp.22-8}. David G.'s brother was

JOHN G. (+1637x). Also served in Muscovy from 1600s as captain and engineer and had a family there. Later royal jeweller and mintmaster in Britain. 1625 proposed to debase English coinage following Russia's example. 1627 reappeared in Moscow with recommendation from King Charles I as mining expert and inventor. A member of Muscovy company, he also engaged in trade. {RGADA, f.150, op.1, 1626, No.7 & 1637, No.1}.

ALEXANDER G. 1697 came to Moscow via Riga and became ensign in P.Gordon's regt. {Gordon, Diary}.

GILCHRIST, JAMES. Died 3/5/1789, St.Petersburg, aged 37. {RBC, I}.

GILLIVRAY. 1913 colonel in (or attached to?) Russian army. {The Tatler, LIII, p.357}.

GILMOUR, or GILMORE, DAVID. 1780s-90s owned a rope-walk in St.Petersburg. {Sb.IRIO, I, 1867, pp.352-61}.

PETER GILLMORE died 6/3/1797 St.Petersburg, aged 47. Another PETER G. married Helen Baillie in Russian capital 1809. {RBC}.

Rev. JAMES GILMOUR (+1892). Born Cathkin near Glasgow. From 1870 missionary in China and Mongolia. Visited Russian Siberia. Wrote "Among the Mongols", L., 1883.

GLAS [Глас] (* ca.1810). Scot by descent, "natural son of Count Douglas". 1830s served in a Russian grenadier regt. with the Eliot brothers. {I.T.Beliayev. Proshloye russkogo izgnannika (unpubl.)}.

GLASGOW. Naval officer. Took part in Russo-Turkish war 1768-1774 {An Authentic Narrative of the Russian Expedition against the Turks by Sea and Land. L., 1772}.

GLASSFORD [Гласфорт], JAMES (+1748,Russia). 1736 joined Russian Navy as lieutenant. Commandant of the port of "Earkee". {OMS, II; Steuart, p.115}.

GLEN [Глен], WILLIAM (1717-1800) died and buried in St.Petersburg. "Mr. Glen" with family of five lived there 1782. {RBC}.

Rev. WILLIAM GLEN. Missionary and philologist. From 1810s worked in Russia, mainly in Astrakhan. Wrote "Journal of a Tour from Astrachan to Karass", Edin., 1823. Translated and published Bible in Persian. Mentioned by writer Aksakov as "Gion". 1833 returned to Britain. {I.S.Aksakov. Pis'ma k rodnym, pp.113-4, 592}.

GORDON [Гордон], ALEXANDER. 1632 capt., regimental quartermaster and company commander under A.Leslie. Fought in Smolensk war as colonel of dragoons 1633-4. His clansmen and comrades-in-arms were Capt. WILLIAM, Ruitmaster ROBERT, Ensign ALEXANDER, Sergeant JAMES and Private THOMAS G. {RGADA, f.210, op.1, No.78}.

PATRICK [Петр Иванович] G. (1635, Auchleuchries, Aberdeenshire-1699, Moscow). General, rear-admiral,chief advisor to Peter the Great, most high-ranking and influential foreigner in Russia of his day. Cadet of the Haddo family. Served Swedish and Polish crowns. 1661 entered Tsar's employ as major with D.Crawford and P.Menzies. 1665 colonel. 1666-7 sent on diplomatic mission from Moscow to London, went to Scotland 1669-70 (when made Freeman of Aberdeen) and 1686. 1677-8 prominent in Chigirin campaigns, made major-gen. and commander of Kiev garrison. Supervised creation of Tsar's Life Guard regiments and initiated military reforms. 1687-9 took part in Crimean campaigns; promoted to full general. 1689 supported Tsar Peter in his coup against Regent Sophia. 1695-6 active in siege and capture of Azov from the Turks. 1698 suppressed Streltsy rebellion saving the throne for Peter. Secured permission to build first Roman Catholic church in Russia. Staunch Jacobite, prevented recognition of William of Orange by Tsar. A well-educated man, G. was also Russian correspondent for "London Gazette" and author of famous diary, still inadequately published. {RGVIA - Passages from the Diary of Gen.Patrick Gordon of Auchleuchries. Aberdeen,1859}. His sons and numerous kinsmen made their mark in Russia.

His eldest son JOHN (1666 or 7, Moscow-1712, Scotland). Started as ensign in Russian army, never finished studies at Douai and Edinburgh and managed family estate of Auchleuchries near Ellon. 1698 visited Moscow with his wife.

JAMES [Яков], second son, (1668-1722, Moscow). Entered Tsar's army as ensign, studied at Memel and Douai. 1689 badly wounded at Killiekrankie. 1690 back in Moscow, capt. in father's Butyrsky regt. which he later commanded. 1700 captured by Swedes at Narva, but soon escaped and fought in many battles of Great Northern War. Became brigadier and Count of Holy Roman Empire.

THEODORE [Федор], Patrick's third son (1681, Kiev-1739x). Student with Jesuits in Eastern Prussia, then ensign in father's regt.

During Great Northern War promoted to colonel. His son, interpreter at Admiralty College and Academy of Sciences, sold Patrick's diary to Count Stroganov in 1759.

WILLIAM G. (+1692,Reval). Patrick's cousin, nephew of P.Menzies. In Russian service by 1685, served as captain in Kiev. Fell ill and died en route to Scotland. {P.Dukes, "P.Gordon and His Family Circle", SSR, No.10, 1988, pp.19-49}.

HARIE [Андрей] G. Relative of Patrick and Jacobite. 1691 came to Moscow on Duke of Gordon's recommendation and joined Russian army as captain. 1700 Lt.-Col. ANDREY G. was taken by Swedes at Narva, but escaped with a party of Russian prisoners who captured the ship transporting them from Stockholm to Gothenburg in 1711. He married a sister of Patrick's second wife. {Vedomosti vremeni Petra Velikago, II, St.Petersburg, 1906, p.109}.

ALEXANDER G. Younger brother of Thomas G., capt. of "Marr Maid", Aberdeen (later Russian admiral, cf. below). 1691 came to Moscow to stay with Patrick. Later ensign. 1710 THOMAS, son of Capt. Alexander G. (same?), was baptized in British Chapel, Moscow. {RBC, I}.

ALEXANDER G. (1669, Auchintoul-1752, ibid.). After a spell in French army came to Russia 1695 and accepted as major. 1697 colonel. 1700 wounded and seized by Swedes at Narva, but exchanged 1707. 1708 major-gen., sent to Poland in command of Russian infantry corps which he thought "nothing inferior to the best disciplined troops in Europe". Back in Scotland on his father's death 1711. "Out" in 1715, commanded Jacobite center at Sheriffmuir. Married Katherine, daughter of Patrick G. Wrote "History of Peter the Great, Emperor of Russia", 2 vols., Aberdeen, 1755.

GEORGE G. 1690s lieutenant in Russia.

Russian Major GORDON of Pflug's regt. killed near Plotsk late in 1705. {Vedomosti vremeni Petra Velikago, I, p.298}.

THOMAS G. (1662-1741, Kronshtadt). Cousin of Patrick. Capt. of merchant vessels in Aberdeen, then in Scottish Navy. 1715 took part in Jacobite rising. 1717 entered Russian service as commodore. 1719 rear-admiral. 1721 vice-admiral; member of Admiralty College and co-author of "Naval Statute". Commanded port of Kronshtadt from 1724; knight of St.Alexander Nevsky. 1727 full admiral. 1734 led Russian squadron in conquest of Danzig. His son WILLIAM was a naval officer and daughter ANN married Sir Henry Stirling, Bart.

ALEXANDER G. (+1739). Son of the Jacobite John G. of Glenbuchat. 1737 joined Russian Navy as midshipman. Killed in Russo-Turkish war. {OMS, II, p.105; Steuart, p.110}.

WILLIAM G. (+1768,Russia). 1764 joined Russian Navy as lieutenant with S.Greig and other Scots. 1766 capt.-lt. {OMS, III, p.421}.

HENRY G. 1784 came to St.Petersburg as C.Cameron's master stonemason, aged 45. {SSR, No.10, 1988}.

Other Gordons appear in RBC and other Russian sources.   Cf. Aberdeen.

GRAHAM [Граам,фон Грагм,Граххам,Графхам,Графман,Грон, Грахан,Грагам], Count David William (ca. 1639, London-1693, Belgorod). First count in Russian service, though origin of title unclear. Alias Baron of Morphie. Served in Sweden, Spain, Poland, Bavaria and Austria for 22 years. 1679 came to Russia "to see his kinsmen and friends" P.Menzies, P.Gordon and Col.Hamilton.   1682 after repeated petitions accepted by Tsar as major-general.   In command of regt. in Smolensk, Moscow and Belgorod. Took part in Crimean campaigns 1687-9 and made lt.-gen.   Roman Catholic. {P.Gordon, Diary; N.Charykov. Posol'stvo v Rim i sluzhba v Moskve Pavla Meneziya, passim}.

MUNGO G., or GRAEME, of Garvock.   Nephew of Sir Henry Stirling, Bart. 1730s apprenticed to G.Napier, merchant in St.Petersburg. Later established his own business in Russia. {SRO GD 24/1/454; Steuart ,p.114}.

WILLIAM G. (+1761,St.Petersburg) married Helena "Skatzcof" in 1758. {RBC}.

General THOMAS G., Lord Lynedoch of Balgowan (1748-1843) and his cousin ROBERT G. visited St.Petersburg and Moscow 1817.

GRANT [Грантъ], "ANTS".   Served under A.Leslie. 1632 reported ill in Moscow. {RGADA, f.210, op.1, No.78}.

Colonel GRANT.   Took part in Chigirin campaign of 1677 with his regt. {P.Gordon, Diary}.

JOHN G. (+1796,Astrakhan).   1783 lieutenant in Russian Navy. 1788 capt.-lt.; fought against Swedes at Oland, Krasnaya Gorka and

Viborg. 1796 sent to Astrakhan, commanded five transports in the Caspian. {OMS, III, pp.428-9}.

GRANT. Noblemen of Vitebsk and Kharkov regions, apparently of Scots origin. {RGIA, f.1343, op.19, No.3923}.

MICHAEL G. married Sarah Baldwin in St.Petersburg 1785. {RBC}.

GRANT. 1870s Scots merchant in charge of telegraph service in Kiakhta on Mongolian border. {J.Gilmour. Among the Mongols. L., 1883}.

LILIAS G. From Inverness. 1916 with E.Moir member of 75-strong unit of Scottish Women's Hospitals. Via Archangel,Moscow and Odessa went to work in field hospitals in Russian lines on Balkan front. {Scots in Russia. Edin., 1987, p.84}.

GRAY [Грай,Грей]. Ruitmaster GILBERT G. and JOHN G. were in A.Leslie's regt. in Moscow 1632. {RGADA, f.210, op.1, No.78}.

JOHN G. 1784 came to St.Petersburg as master plasterer, aged 35, to work with C.Cameron. {SSR, No.10, 1988, pp.59-60, 71}.

GREIG [Грейг], SAMUEL [Самуил Карлович] (1735, Inverkeithing-1788, Reval). Son of Fife shipmaster. With Royal Navy in Seven Years' War. 1764 with C.Douglas and other Scots enlisted for Russian service as capt. of 1st rank. Prominent in Mediterranean campaign against Turks and battle of Chesme 1770, made rear-admiral. 1775 vice-admiral and Commander of Kronshtadt. 1777 returned to Scotland to become Freeman of Edinburgh. 1782 admiral, supervised reconstruction of Kronshtadt and armament of the Navy. Paved the way of many Scots to Russia, notably C.Gascoigne and possibly C.Cameron, as well as seamen. 1788 headed Baltic fleet in war with Sweden and won battle of Hogland, but died of fever on board his ship. He was knight of several Russian orders and had a state funeral. {TsGAVMF, f.8; A.G.Cross, "Samuel Greig, Catherine the Great's Scottish Admiral", Mariner's Mirror, LX, No.3, 1974}. His sons ALEXIS, JOHN, SAMUEL and CHARLES all held ranks in Russian Navy and had training in Britain. The eldest

ALEXIS [Алексей Самуилович] (1775-1845). Midshipman soon after birth. 1785 lieutenant and father's aide. 1798-1800 in Russo-British expedition against the French. 1805 rear-admiral. 1813 led squadron at capture of Danzig, became vice-admiral and Russian citizen. 1816 appointed Commander of Black Sea Fleet, Governor of Sevastopol and Nikolaev. 1828-9 fought in Turkish war, admiral after conquest of Anapa. A formidable scholar, he directed the construction of Pulkovo observatory near St.Petersburg. {Yu.S.Kriuchkov. Alexey Samuilovich Greig. Moscow, 1984}. His son

SAMUEL [Самуил Алексеевич] (1827-1887). After distinguished career in the Guards and Naval Ministry became State Controller 1874 and Minister of Finance 1878-80.

Family survived into 20th century and matriculated their coat of arms 1915. {RGIA, f.1343, op.35, No.6406 & f.1689}.

GRIEVE [Гриве,Греве], JAMES (ca.1710-1763). 1733 M.D., Edinburgh. 1734 moved to Russia and held various medical posts. 1747 City Physician to St.Petersburg. 1753 fellow of Royal College of Physicians of Edinburgh. Also doctor to Russian Court. Produced first translation of "History of Kamchatka" by S.P.Krasheninnikov (Gloucester, 1764). {Caledonian Phalanx, p.51}.

JOHN [Иван Яковлевич] G. (1753, Edinburgh-1805, St.Petersburg). Related to James. Studied Edinburgh and Glasgow. 1778 became army doctor in Russia with help from Dr.Rogerson. 1783 returned to Britain, was elected member of many learned societies. Wrote first Western work on fermented mare's milk, "An Account of ... Koumiss, with Observations on its Use in Medicine" (Transactions of Royal Soc. of Edinburgh, 1788). 1798 back in Russia, court physician to Emperors Paul and Alexander I. His children were born in St.Petersburg with Emperor and his family as godparents. Tradition has it that G. was poisoned by a rival doctor. His elder sister JOAN married Dr. J.Mounsey. {RBC}.

GRUBB, DAVID. 1784 arrived in St.Petersburg, aged 36, as one of C.Cameron's stonemasons. Headed successful petition to erect Imperial Scottish Lodge of St.Petersburg (No.207 in Roll of Grand Lodge of Scotland), the only one in Russia to consist of working, not symbolic, masons. His Russian-born children: DAVID (*1785), CATHERINE (*1787) and WILLIAM (*1788). {RBC, I; SSR, No.10, 1988, pp.64,71}.

GUILD, WILLIAM (+1685,Russia). 1661 entered Russian service with A.Burnett and other Scots. Promoted to lt.-colonel. {P.Gordon, Diary}.

GUTHRIE [Гутри,Гютри], THOMAS.   Served in A.Leslie's regt. 1632. {RGADA, f.210, op.1, No.78}.

MATTHEW G. (1743, Edinburgh-1807, St.Petersburg).   Scion of falconers of Kings of Scots, lairds of Hawkerstoun near Forfar. Studied Edinburgh. 1769 army doctor in Russia, took part in Turkish war. 1778 to his death chief doctor to Land (First) Cadet Corps. 1793 confirmed his hereditary noble status; rose to State Councillor.   His interests spanned botany, zoology, ethnology, history, geography, mineralogy, literature etc., and he contributed many articles to "The Bee" magazine. Member of Russia's first musical society in St.Petersburg, founder-member of Royal Society of Edinburgh and elected to many other learned bodies. Translated and published first piece of Russian fiction to appear in English, Empress Catherine's tale "Ivan Czarewitz, or The Rose without Prickles that Stings Not", 1793. Wrote "Dissertations sur les Antiquites de Russie" describing Russian customs, games, songs etc., and edited his wife's "A Tour... through the Taurida, or Crimea", 1802. His daughter ANASTASIA-JESSY married 1) C.Gascoigne and 2) T.Bonar; other daughters were MARIA HELLENA (*+1784) and MARY (*1789). {RNL, f.949, Nos.13-5, 43; RBC; Caledonian Phalanx, pp.55-9}.

HAIG, HAGUE. JAMES HAIG (*1756). Worked in Russia from 1784 as C.Cameron's stonemason. {SSR, No.10, 1988}.

MARY HAGUE, widow, married Alexander Dalgleish in St.Petersburg 1828. {RBC, II}.

HALDANE [ГольденЁ], JAMES. 1716-7 British Minister Resident in Russia, attended Peter the Great in Amsterdam and probably had commissions from the Tsar. 1723 Russian students in Britain were to be sent home by "the English merchant Goldan". {Soloviev, IX, p.481}.

ALEXANDER HALDEN. C.Cameron's bricklayer. 1784 came to St.Petersburg, aged 35. {SSR, No.10, 1988}.

HALIBURTON [Галибуртон] see Stewart.

HALLIDAY [Галлидей], MATTHEW (1732 Lochbrow, Dumfriesshire-1809, St.Petersburg). Doctor, in Russia by 1758. Physician to Chancellor Count M.I. Vorontsov. 1771 took effective measures against plague in Moscow and Yaroslavl. From 1780 directed St.Petersburg Inoculation Hospital and personally inoculated members of Imperial family, for which he was made State Councillor 1799. He left a large family, and St.Petersburg island of Goloday was probably named after them.

WILLIAM [Василий Матвеевич] H. (1759-1825). Eldest son of Matthew. Studied Edinburgh, London and Tubingen. From 1785 practised in both Russian capitals and provincial towns of Rylsk and Bronnitsy. Retired as State Councillor. His brother

MICHAEL (*1765,St.Petersburg). Trained in British Navy. 1789 entered Russian service as lieutenant and took part in Swedish war. 1791 resigned. {OMS, III}. His brother

JOHN (1773-1845x). Merchant in St.Petersburg. 1832 unsuccessfully claimed noble status. Had seven children. {RGIA, f.1343, op.19, No.2534}.

ANDREW H. (1781, Dumfries-1839, ibid.). Obviously related to Russian branch. After graduating from Edinburgh (M.D.,1806) visited Russia. Served with Wellington's army in Portugal and at Waterloo. 1821 knighted as court physician. {DNB, VIII, pp.994-5}.

HALLOWAY, or GALLOWAY [Гал(л)овей], CHRISTOPHER (+1645x). Builder, clockmaker and waterworks expert. 1621 came to Russia and employed in Moscow Kremlin for over 20 years. 1623-5 completed Spassky gate tower and installed first clock there, decorating the spire with naked allegorical figures which had to be dressed by Tsar's order! 1633 he designed Kremlin's water system. 1644 discovered silver and copper ore in the Urals. {RGADA, ff.141, 150, 396; Steuart, p.42}.

HAMEL [Гамель], JOSEPH [Иосиф Христианович]. Of German descent. Doctor to Russian Court and academician. Ca. 1850 worked in English and Scottish archives. Wrote "Englishmen in Russia in 16th and 17th centuries", St.Petersburg, 1865-9, first work on Russo-British contacts. {SRO GD 268/87/1}.

HAMILTON [Гамильтон]. One of the earliest and most famous Scottish names in Russia. It is said that THOMAS H., a cadet of the lordly family, came to Muscovy with his son PETER and daughter "AVDOTYA" in 1542. Peter's son GRIGORY is recorded as nobleman of Novgorod 1611. His daughter
EVDOKIA GRIGORYEVNA H. (+1672,Moscow) married Boyar Artamon Matveyev who directed Russia's foreign policy under Tsar Alexey. Their son was Andrey Matveyev, first permanent Russian ambassador to Britain 1707-8, and their ward was Natalya Naryshkina, Peter the Great's mother. Evdokia's niece
EVDOKIA (AVDOTYA) PETROVNA H. married Fedor Naryshkin, Tsarina Natalya's uncle. 1676-82 she was exiled with her "foreign mother" and children, but was revered by Old Believers of Arzamas as "the holy woman Deborah". Her relative
MARY [Мария Даниловна] H. (1690s-1719). Lady in waiting to Catherine, Peter the Great's wife. She became mistress of Peter's aide and possibly of the Tsar himself and was beheaded in St.Petersburg for murdering her child. Her story strangely resembles the Scots ballad "Queen's Marie".
The family gradually became russified as KHOMUTOVS and produced many outstanting men in military and civil service, notably General MIKHAIL GRIGORYEVICH KHOMUTOV (1795-1864), hero of numerous campaigns and first leader ("Ataman") of Don Cossacks who was not a Cossack by birth. {RGIA, f.1343, op.19, Nos.518-21 &

op.31, Nos.2846-54; Dvoriansky adres-kalendar' na 1898 god, St.Petersburg, pp.197-201}. Besides them countless other Hamiltons appear in Russia.

Lt.-Colonel (?) JOHN H. 1629 came to Moscow with his wife after two years in Sweden. Received pay in money and kind and 500 serfs. 1632-4 fought at Smolensk. {Stashevsky, Smolenskaya voyna}.

Lt. ANDREY (Andrew or Henry) H. 1647 came to enter Tsar's employ with Col.Urie and others. {RGADA,.f.150,.op.1,.1647,.No.27}.

Col. ALEXANDER H. served from 1640s. 1650 sent with his regt. to quell rebellion at Pskov {Olearius}. ANDREY H. also appears as Russian colonel in 1650s. {RGADA, f.141, op.3, No.55}.

Ensign ALEXANDER H. came to join Muscovite army from Holland in July 1661. {RGADA, f.150, Op.1, 1661, No.16}.

JOHN H. 1661 arrived in Moscow with P.Gordon and enlisted as ensign in D.Crawford's regiment. 1678 Capt. John H. was wounded in 2nd Chigirin campaign. Lt.-Col. HAMILTON (same?), a Roman Catholic, died 1693 in Belgorod entrusting his sons JOHN and PATRICK to Gordon's care; 1697 John became ensign in Gordon's Butyrsky regt. {P.Gordon, Diary}.

ALEXANDER HAMILTON, lt.-col. in Russia, obtained birth-brief from Privy Council of Scotland 1670. He was eldest son of Sir Alexander H. of Fenton and Innerwick, East Lothian. 1681 he was back in Scotland and petitioned for rank of major in the militia. {J.M.Hartley, Guide to Documents and Manuscripts in the UK Relating to Russia, 1987, p.82}.

Col. HAMILTON, a friend of P.Gordon and D.Graham, served in Russia from 1670s. He died in Sevsk 1689. {P.Gordon, Diary}.

IVAN H. Commanded infantry regt. in St.Petersburg garrison under R.Bruce and defended the newly-built city against Swedes 1705. {Ustrialov, IV}.

Baron HUGO JOHAN H. (1660s-1748). Swedish general. 1709 captured at Poltava and kept in custody by his "compatriot", Russian Gen. J.D.Bruce. Spent many years in Moscow and Kirillov monastery. 1722 returned to Sweden to become field marshal.

PETER H. 1715 hired as lieutenant, but acted as translator and interpreter for Admiralty College. Mentioned 1725. {OMS, I, p.90}.

Master plasterer JOHN, aged 37, and plasterer ARCHIBALD H., aged 20, came to Russia 1784 to work under C.Cameron. ANN, daughter of the former, was baptized in St.Petersburg 1785, and the latter died there 1799. {SSR, No.10, 1988; RBC, I}.

GEORGE MONTAGUE [Егор Андреевич] H. (1765 or 6-1841, St.Petersburg). 1791 capt.-lt. in Black Sea fleet. 1809 capt. of 1st rank. 1824 rear-admiral. 1829 vice-admiral, commanded 3rd Naval Division in Kronshtadt. Knight of St.Anne, 1st class, St.Vladimir, 2nd cl. and St.George, 4th cl. Had issue. {OMS, III, p.349; RBC}.

Lord ALEXANDER H. (1767-1852). 1807 British Ambassador in Russia until relations broke off after Russo-French treaty of Tilsit. Later 10th Duke of H.

Cf. Douglas-Hamilton and Selkirk.

HARDIE, JAMES (+1777, aged 41). 1772 married Catherine Stokes in St.Petersburg; had daughter AGNES (*1773). {RBC}.

JAMES H. Smith. 1784 came to Russia, aged 26, to work under C.Cameron. {SSR, No.10, 1988}.

HASTIE [Гесте], WILLIAM [Василий Иванович] (1754-1832, Tsarskoye Selo). 1784 arrived in St.Petersburg as C.Cameron's stonemason. Set out to work on his own after the Empress praised his drawings. 1795 chief architect of Ekaterinoslav and Crimea, restored Khan's Palace in Bakhchisaray. 1801 involved in reconstruction of Izhorsky foundry at Kolpino under C.Gascoigne. Designed new cast-iron bridges in St.Petersburg. From 1808 chief architect of Tsarskoye Selo. Drew up city plans for Moscow, Kiev, Saratov, Tomsk, Penza, Smolensk etc. Married Margaret Bryce. {M.Korshunova, "William Hastie in Russia", Architectural History, XVII, 1974}.

HASTIE. Wealthy Scots family in Moscow, 19th-early 20th cent. CHARLES H. (1845-1919, Moscow). 1904 supervised construction of St.Andrew's House for British governesses in Moscow, founded by his sister JANE McGILL. Wrote "Handbook for Members of Congregation" of St.Andrew's, Moscow (publ.1908). {H.Pitcher, The Smiths of Moscow}.

HAY [Гай,Гей], D(avid?). "Nobleman's son" from Edinburgh. 1630 enlisted in Tsar's army and evidently fought in Smolensk war 1632-4. {Stashevsky, Smolenskaya voyna}.

THOMAS H. 1650s-60s officer in Muscovy. King Charles II asked the Tsar to release him, but outcome unknown. {Phipps, p.306}.

WILLIAM H. 1661 joined P.Gordon and others in Pskov and came to Moscow to become lieutenant in D.Crawford's regt. 1670s major. Wounded during defence of Chigirin 1678.

Capt. HAY. 1688 married in Moscow, but died shortly. {P.Gordon, Diary}.

WILLIAM H. Jacobite. 1718 joined Russian Navy as capt. of 1st rank. Commanded warships "Varakhail", "Moskva" and "St.Alexander". Captured a Swedish transport. 1724 dismissed. {OMS, I, p.94}.

JOHN H. 1725 Jacobite envoy in St.Petersburg where he stayed for some months. {Hist. MSS Commission.Report on the MSS of the Earl of Eglinton. L., 1885, pp.175-6}.

GEORGE H. died and buried 1763, St.Petersburg. JOHN and ROBERT H. both married in Russian capital 1776, and Robert died there 1802, aged 69. {RBC}.

"GELENUS" H. (ca.1764-1789). 1784 entered Russian service as midshipman. 1785 lietenant. Killed in sea battle with Swedes at Rochensalm. {OMS, III, p.338}.

HENDERSON [Гендерсон]. "ELIS" and "MATS" H. served under A.Leslie 1632. {RGADA, f.210, op.1, No.78}.

JOHN H. 1660s lieutenant in Tsar's army. {P.Gordon, Diary}.

WILLIAM H. (+1718,Moscow). Early member of British congregation in Moscow by 1709. {RBC}.

SCOTT H. 1771 midshipman in Russian Navy, took part in Mediterranean campaign against Turks. 1773 resigned. {OMS, III, p.361}.

LOGAN H. 1786 came to Russia from Paris with two sisters named Kirkland, allegedly his nieces, but the elder was his mistress. Signed contract to manage Prince Potemkin's botanic garden in Crimea, but soon denounced as impostor. {A.G.Cross, "The British in Catherine's Russia", p.262}.

Rev. EBENEZER H. (*1784, near Dunfermline). Missionary with British and Foreign Bible Society. Worked in Scandinavia with J.Paterson. In Russia from 1812. Co-founder of Russian Bible Society. An able linguist, he supervised Bible translations into Oriental languages.

Wrote "Biblical Researches and Travels in Russia", 1826. {C.R.Bawden. Shamans, Lamas and Evangelicals. L., 1985}.

HENDRIE (?) [Гендрик], JAMES. "Nobleman's son" from Stirling. 1630 came to Russia to serve in her army. Probably fought the Poles at Smolensk 1632-4. {Stashevsky, Smolenskaya voyna}.

HEWITT, JAMES. Councillor of Commerce in St.Petersburg. His will is dated 15/1/1747. {SRO}.
WILLIAM H., M.D. Buried 17/8/1766, St.Petersburg. {RBC}.

HOPE. A."OP" officer in Russian army, involved in Smolensk war 1632-4. {Stashevsky, Smolenskaya voyna}.
JAMES, Lord H. 1777 visited Russia with his wife Elizabeth and was graciously received by Empress Catherine. Brought back to Britain for the first time two medicinal assafoetida plants, sent by M.Guthrie to Royal Botanic Garden, Edinburgh. Later Earl of Hopetoun. {Caledonian Phalanx, pp.58-9}.

HOPPER [Гоппер]. Prominent Scots family in Moscow, latter 19th-early 20th century. WILLIAM H. and his four sons owned Hopper's Machine Works in Moscow. 1886 their attempt to introduce rugby to Russia failed when the police found the game too violent. {Pitcher, Smiths of Moscow}.

HUME, or HOME [Юм], ROBERT. Mentioned as Capt. Robert "Hoim" at muster of Leslie's regt. in Moscow 1632. Promoted to lt.-col.during War of Smolensk. 1633 col.Matheson in his will bequeathed to H. his "sattin suit, scarlett cloakc and bcst sword". {RGADA, f.210, op.1, No.78; Scottish Soldier Abroad, p.54}.
Ensign "YURGEN" (GEORGE) H. also served in Muscovy under A.Leslie 1632.
DANIEL DOUGLAS H. (1833-1886). Spiritist, held seances in Russia. Mentioned in A.I.Herzen's letter to I.S.Turgenev 24/5/1860. V.S.Soloviev met him in London and called him "the founder of modern spiritism". {Perepiska I.S.Turgeneva. Moscow, 1986}.

HUNTER [Гунтерĕ], DAVID. 1829 married Maria Lithgow in St.Petersburg and had issue. {RBC}.

HYNDFORD [Гиндфорд], JOHN CARMICHAEL, 3rd Earl of (1701, Edinburgh-1767, Lanarkshire). Served in British army. 1737 inherited title. 1744-9 British Ambassador in St.Petersburg. Intrigued against J.Keith forcing him to leave Russia. Empress Catherine called him "a complete drunkard", but "a man with common sense". On retirement took to agriculture and used Russian seeds for his plantations. {Memoirs of Catherine the Great; DNB, III, pp.1039-40}.

INGLIS [Инглис], JOHN. Officer in Muscovite army, early 17th century. {RIB, XXVIII}.

PETER I. "Master of perspective painting". 1670s assisted pastor Gregory on Russia's first theatre productions at court of Tsar Alexey, using Biblical and mythological subjects. Possibly also Tsar's gardener. {RGADA, f.141; Soloviev, VII, p.132}.

GEORGE I. (+ca.1665). Colonel, served in Ukraine with his regt. {P.Gordon, Diary}. His widow married W.Bruce, and his sons probably were:

IVAN YURYEVICH (JOHN) I. 1678 captain, took part in 2nd Chigirin campaign. {Charykov, p.361}.

ANDREY YURYEVICH I. Colonel. From 1701 commanded infantry regiment which bore his name (later Viborg regt.). 1704 active in capture and fortification of Narva. 1705-6 commanded garrison at Ivangorod. Corresponded with his half-brothers the Bruces. 1709 infantry colonel I. (same?) wounded at Poltava. {Artillery Museum Archive, St.Petersburg, f.2, op.1, No.6}.

DAVID YURYEVICH I. 1692 captain in Bombardier company, Preobrazhensky Guards. 1697 one of noblemen with Tsar Peter's "Great Embassy" to the West. {Ustrialov, III, pp.7, 572}.

FEDOR I. 1786-96 page at court of Empress Catherine. His pay was 114 roubles. {RNL, f.855, No.2}.

THOMAS I. Engineer. 1794 proposed to reconstruct St.Petersburg Arsenal and works at Briansk, but failed in his task. {V.Rodzevich. Istoricheskoe opisanie St.Peterburgskago Arsenala. SPb., 1914, pp.138-41}.

ARCHIBALD I. 28/2/1825 died in St.Petersburg, aged 65. {RBC}.

INNES [Иннес] (+ca.1738). From Aberdeen. Lieutenant in Russian Horse Guards. During Turkish war of 1735-9 rose to colonel of dragoons. J.Cook called him "brave I., the soldiers' friend, and beloved of all good men". Fell in battle. {Steuart, p.115}.

THOMAS I. of Learney. 1837 visited Russia including the great fair at Nizhny Novgorod. Colonel in Gordon Highlanders {information from his great-grandson, Sir Malcolm Innes, Lyon King of Arms}.

JAMES I. Native of Lossiemouth. Sailor on schooner "Venture" of Elgin (Capt.Alexander Walker). 1856 died of cholera in St.Petersburg, aged 19. {RBC, IV}.

IRVINE, IRVING [Ирвин(г)]. JAMES IRVING, "musketeer captain", served in A.Leslie's regt. 1632. {RGADA, f.210, op.1, No.78}.

DAVID and WALTER IRVINE, stonemasons and possibly cousins, aged 25, came to Russia on invitation of C.Cameron 1784. 1804 the former assisted Cameron in his work for the Admiralty, the latter died in St.Petersburg 1823. {RBC; SSR, No.10, 1988}.

WILLIAM I. 1880s Russian Vice-Consul in Lerwick, Shetland. {Adres-Kalendar'. Obshchaya Rospis'. 1884}.

ITALINSKY [Италинский], ANDREY YAKOVLEVICH (1742 or 3, near Lubny, Poltava region-1827, Rome). Son of village priest. Studied medicine at Leiden. 1774 came to Edinburgh where he spent about a year perfecting his knowledge. Attended J.Black's lectures and became honorary member of Medical Society. Later Russian Ambassador in Naples, Constantinople and Rome. A remarkable linguist and connoisseur of arts, he was called "first Russian archaeologist" by A.I.Turgenev. {RBS, "I-K", pp.151-2; Cross, By the Banks, p.138}.

JAMES. 11/1591 King James VI asked Queen Elizabeth of England to write to the Tsar on behalf of Scots captain named J. who has long been imprisoned in Muscovy. His fate is unknown, but he probably joined Tsar's army, as did J.Lingett and G.Elphinstone. 1591 there were about 150 Scots mercenaries in Russia. {Hist. MSS Commission.Portland Manuscripts. L., 1890, II, p.18; Steuart, p.20}.

JOHNSTON [Джонстон], WILLIAM. Colonel. 1656 came to serve Tsar with T.Dalyell and W.Drummond. 1658 received safe-conduct for his wife to go to their children in Scotland after his mother-in-law died. 1659 helped Drummond to take revenge on a German merchant who insulted Scots. {RGADA, f.141, op.3, No.32; P.Gordon, Diary}.

GEORGE J. 1656-7 captain, commanded a company in Dalyell's regt. at Polotsk. Probably related to Colonel J. {RGADA, f.396, op.1, No.53200}.

Colonel WILLIAM J. Brother of Marquis of Annandale, Jacobite. 1710 went to Russia with recommendation to R.Erskine from Duke of

Marlborough and Dr.Ch.Oliphant {Academy of Sciences Archive, St.Petersburg, f.120/1, No.120}.

JOHN J. 1710 applied for safe-conduct to go from Danzig to Russia. {SRO, GD 27/3/2}.

Col. JOHNSTON from "Kenneil" served in Russia 1730s-40s. {Steuart, p.115}.

JOHN GLEN J. 1800s lived in St.Petersburg with his wife Mary and children. {RBC}.

R.JOHNSTON. Wrote "Travels through Part of the Russian Empire", L., 1817.

JONES [Джонс], JOHN PAUL (1747, Kirkbean, Kirkcudbright-1792, Paris). Settled in Virginia and won fame with young American Navy during War of Independence. 1788 invited into Russian service and promoted to rear-admiral of Black Sea fleet. He took part in two victorious battles with the Turks near Ochakov, which earned him the order of St.Anne,1st class, but soon lost command through mistrust and intrigues of rivals. He languished for nearly three years in St.Petersburg, then went back to France. J. was greatly esteemed by Field Marshal Suvorov, and his early death was regretted by Napoleon who believed he could have defeated the English on sea. {RGADA, f.168; Istorichesky Vestnik, LXXXII,1902, No.3; S.E.Morison.John Paul Jones. Boston, 1959}.

KATTI-GHERY KRIM-GHERY [Крым-Гирей] ALEXANDER. Descendant of Crimean Khans, styled "Sultan". Converted to Christianity by Scots missionaries at Karras and sent to Edinburgh to study 1820. There he married Anne Neilson of Millbank. Their daughter Alexandrina was baptized in St.Petersburg 1821. {RBC; Steuart, p.135}.

KAYSAROV [Кайсаров], ANDREY SERGEYEVICH (1782-1813). Son of landowner from Yaroslavl. After some time in the army studied at Gottingen University with A.I.Turgenev. 1806-8 lived in Britain including Edinburgh where the univesity gave him a doctorate. Also became Freeman of Dumfries. 1810-3 professor of Russian in Dorpt. 1812 initiated and directed Russian army print. Killed in battle with the French near Bauzen. {Syn Otechestva, 1813, No.25, pp.237-40}.

KEDDIE, FRANK. Young Scot who came in summer 1917 to work with Quaker mission at Buzuluk in Samara region. He had "a shrewd business head", quickly learned Russian, bought all necessities for the unit and organized campaign against rodents that damaged crops. 1918 arrested and nearly shot by Red Guard. {R.C.Scott, Quakers in Russia. L., 1964}.

KEIR [Кейр,Кир], NICHOLAS. 1647 soldier who was hired in Holland and came to Moscow via Archangel with G.Garioch, J.Stewart and W.Bruce.
JAMES [Яков Вильгельмович] K. 1806-38 chief doctor at Count Sheremetev's Hospital in Moscow. 1817 professor of Medico-Chirurgical Academy headed by J.Wylie. {P.V.Vlasov. Obitel' miloserdiya. Moscow, 1991, pp.59-60}. "The Russian Troubadour" by B.Beresford (L., 1816) contains a "Dirge to the Memory of Mrs.Kier of Moscow", probably related to him.

KEITH [Кейт]. An officer of that name was in Russian service by 1624. {Steuart, p.32}.
Lt.-Col. WILLIAM K. 1632 enrolled in Muscovite army with a salary of 75 roubles. He took part in Smolensk war and campaigns against Crimean Tartars and became colonel. At muster of Leslie's regt. in Moscow he was joined by Major ANDREW, Capt. ALBERT K. and a NICHOLAS "KET". {RGADA, f.210, op.1, No.78}.

GEORGE K. (+1650s,Russia). Lt.-colonel who served in Ireland and Muscovy. Younger brother of Robert K. of Kindruct. His relative was probably JULIANA K. whose wedding to Lt.-Col. Winram in Moscow in 1663 was witnessed by P.Gordon. {Birthbrieves from Registers of the Burgh of Aberdeen, Spalding Club Misc., VIII, p.340; P.Gordon, Diary}.

Ruitmaster GEORGE K. 1661 came to Moscow with other Scots from Swedish service on P.Gordon's advice. 1666 mentioned by Gordon on latter's departure to Britain. {RGADA, f.150, op.1, 1661, No.33}.

Shipwright "IAN CORNILIS" K. "from Kazan". 1703-4 worked at Lodeynoe Pole wharf. {Ustrialov, IV, Pt.1, p.247}.

JAMES FRANCIS EDWARD [Яков Вилимович] K. (1696, Inverugie near Peterhead-1758, Hochkirchen,Germany). 2nd son of 9th Earl Marischal. Involved in Jacobite risings 1715 and 1719. Studied in Paris and served in Spanish army. 1717 tried to enter Russian service and succeeded in 1728 as major-general on recomendation of Duke of Liria. Played leading role in wars with Poland 1733-5, Turkey 1735-9 and Sweden 1741-3. Rose to full general, knight of St.Andrew, Governor of Ukraine and Ambassador to Stockholm. One of Russia's first freemasons, became Provincial Grand Master. His brother GEORGE, 10th Earl Marischal (1693-1778) visited him in Russia and applied to Empress Elizabeth for citizenship; when it was refused K. left St.Petersburg for Prussian service 1747. King Frederick made him field marshal and Governor of Berlin. Killed in battle with Austrians. {RGADA, ff.96, 177, 179, 181, 187; RGVIA, ff.410, 460, 461; A Fragment of a Memoir of Field Marschal Keith written by himself. Aberdeen, 1843}.

Sir ROBERT K., 5th Baronet of Ludquhairn. Served with his cousin J.Keith in Russian army for 15 years fighting in Polish, Turkish and Swedish campaigns. Married Margaret von Suchin, daughter of Saxon envoy in St.Petersburg. {Steuart, p 113}

ROBERT K. (+1774,Edinburgh). Son of Colonel K. of Craig. 1758-62 British Minister in Russia. {Memoirs of Catherine the Great; DNB, X, pp.1216-7}.

KELLIE [Келли], DAVID. "Lieutenant of the Scottish Land" engaged by A.Leslie. Arrived in Moscow 1630. {RGADA, f.150, op.1, 1630, No.4}.

KENNEDY [Кеннеди]. 1665 a Scot named K. came to Moscow with Dr.Wilson, and possibly was a physician himself. On the way back he was given letters by Scots officers in Tsar's employ, but lost them in a "fitt of frensy" at Riga. {P.Gordon, Diary}.

LUKE K. (+1722,Moscow). "Bombardier" hired in England by Tsar Peter's "Great Embassy" 1698. Served under J.Bruce. Advanced to lt.-col. of artillery. Burial of his son JAMES in Moscow 23/1/1706 was the first ceremony performed in British Chapel in Russia. {Ustrialov, III, p.581; RBC, I}.

JAMES K. (ca.1694-1760, St.Petersburg). 1714 sub-lieutenant in Russian navy. 1724 capt.-lt. 1734 in Danzig expedition under Admiral Gordon. 1752 rear-admiral, commander of Reval squadron and member of Admiralty College. 1757 retired as vice-admiral. {OMS, I, pp.171-4}.

SARAH [Сара Ивановна] (or Mary?) K. 1st "kammer-frau" of Empress Maria, wife of Paul I. Lived in Mikhailovsky Palace in St.Petersburg when Paul was assassinated there. Her granddaughter, a Ms.Henderson, was nurse to Smirnova-Rosset's children. {A.O.Smirnova-Rosset. Dnevnik. Vospominaniya..M.,.1989,.pp.468,.567-8,.741}.

JOHN K. Lieutenant in British artillery, "a tall handsome Scot". Ca. 1915 member of military mission to Russia where he made friends with Russian officer Beliayev whose mother was an Elliot. {I.T.Beliayev. Proshloye russkogo izgnannika, p.252 (unpublished)}.

KENNETH [Кеннет], ANTHONY. 1632 ruitmaster in A.Gordon's company of A.Leslie's regt. {RGADA, f.210, op.1, No.78}.

KENZIE [Кензи], WILLIAM. 1734 enlisted in Navy as capt. of 1st rank; in Danzig campaign under Adm.Gordon. Took part in Russo-Turkish war 1735-9. 1740 arrested in Azov with G.Leslie for disobedience to Vice-Adm. Bredal, tried in St.Petersburg and dismissed "for obstinacy" 1741.

Another WILLIAM K., apparently related to above, 1737 lieutenant, sent to Ochakov during Turkish war. Left Russian service by 1742. {OMS, II, pp.173-4}.

KER(R). Mrs. KERR lived in Moscow ca. 1800. Her imposing house stood at the corner of Kadashevsky Embankment and Polianka St.

and was damaged by fire 1812. {Pamiatniki arkhitektury Moskvy, IV, 1994, p.26}.

CHARLES KERR's marriage to Mary Anne Seymour in 1815 was the first ceremony in new British Church in St.Petersburg. Their Russian-born sons were JOHN (*1816) and ROBERT (*1818). {RBC, II}.

DAVID KER (1842-1914). Cheshire-born Scot. 1867 went to Russia as tutor to Miliutin family. Correspondent for "Daily Telegraph" and "New York Herald" with Russian army; in Khiva expedition 1873 and Turkish war 1877-8. Wrote novels on Russian history. {H.Pitcher, "From a Tutor's Journal", SSR, No.10, 1988, pp.165-76}.

Cf. Carr.

KILBURN, JAMES. 1830s lived in St.Petersburg. Had issue by his wife Ann. {RBC, II}.

KINLOCH [Кинлох], WILLIAM. Officer in Muscovite army, 17th cent. {RIB, XXVIII}.

ALEXANDER K. died 1841, aged 40, St.Petersburg. Kinlochs who lived in Russian capital and Kronshtadt were related to Carricks. MARIA YAKOVLEVNA K. died 1903. {RBC; SSR, No.1, 1983, p.74}.

KINNAIRD [Кинарт], JAMES. 1613 one of Scots in Polish garrison at Belaya who went over to Russians. 1632-4 fought against former employers at Smolensk. {Stashevsky, Smolenskaya voyna}.

KINNEAR, GEORGINA (1826-1914, Edinburgh). Governess in family of Lord Napier in St.Petersburg 1860-4, then with the Miliutins. She was well-educated and spoke fluent French, German and Russian. {SSR, No.10, 1988, pp.167-8}.

KINNINMONT [Кинемонд], PATRICK. Colonel in Russian army by 1629. Took part in Smolensk war 1632-4. {T.Urquhart, The Jewel, p.139; Stashevsky, Smolenskaya voyna}.

Col. JOHN K. 1630s Swedish Governor of Noteborg (Oreshek), Russian border fortress taken by Swedes. 1636 obtained birth-brief from Privy Council of Scotland. {Steuart, p.40}.

KORSAKOV [Корсаков], NIKOLAY IVANOVICH (1749-1788). Engineer officer, first Russian to study canal construction abroad. 1776 after a spell at Oxford came to Scotland on recommendation of Russian Consul Baxter. Based for three months in Glasgow receiving Freedom of the burgh, visited Edinburgh, Forth & Clyde Canal site and Carron works, met R.Mackell, J.Watt and J.Robison. Back in Russia, he worked in St.Petersburg, Kherson and newly-founded Sevastopol under Rear-Adm. Mackenzie, but not as canal-builder. 1786 colonel. Lost his life at siege of Ochakov during Turkish war. {RSL, f.137; A.G.Cross, "A Russian Engineer in 18th-century Britain", SEER, LV, 1977}.

KROPOTKIN [Кропоткин], Prince PIOTR ALEXEYEVICH (1842-1921). Anarchist revolutionary, geographer and geologist. 1874 arrested for socialist activity. 1876 escaped from military hospital in St.Petersburg and spent several weeks hiding in Edinburgh under the name Levashov. While there he wrote articles on geography for "The Times" and "Nature" magazine, but as he learned English from scholarly books only his Scots hostess could hardly understand him. Emigre until 1917. {P.A.Kropotkin. Zapiski revolutsionera. M., 1988, pp.368-73}.

LAING [Ланг], GILBERT (+1777, aged 48, St.Petersburg). Merchant. 1765 married Elizabeth Gardner in St.Petersburg. Their children were PEGGY (1767-1769) and MARY (*+1769). {RBC, I}.

ARCHIBALD L. 1783 enlisted as lieutenant in Russian Navy. Sent to Astrakhan, commanded a ship in the Caspian. 1786 dismissed. {OMS, IV, p.218}.

JAMES L. Died 1833, aged 34, St.Petersburg {RBC,III}.

LANDELLS, ALEXANDER (+1678, Chigirin). 1661 with W.Airth and other Scots left Swedish service for that of Russia on advice of P.Gordon. Major, then lt.-col. in Gordon's dragoon regt. Killed by Turkish bomb during defence of Chigirin. Also called "Langdales". {P.Gordon, Diary}.

LANGCAKE, MUNGO. Died 1770, St.Petersburg. {RBC, I}.

LAUDER. Ruitmaster WILLIAM "LADOR" served in A.Leslie's regt. and company 1632. {RGADA, f.210, op.1, No.78}.

Lieutenant LAUDER. 1680s served in Russian army. {Gordon, Diary}.

JESSIE L. (1810-1876, St.Petersburg). 1827 married Andrew Carrick and settled with him in Russia. {Caledonian Phalanx, pp.90-105}.

LAURISTON [Лористон], JACQUES-ALEXANDRE-BERNARD (1768, Pondicherry-1828, France). Grand-nephew of famous adventurer and banker John Law of Lauriston near Edinburgh (1671-1729). French artillery general, fought in many campaigns. 1811-2 Napoleon's Ambassador in St.Petersburg, then joined invading French forces; in October 1812 sent from Moscow to Russian Commander-in-Chief Kutuzov to negotiate peace, but did not succeed. 1813 commanded a corps at Leipzig where taken prisoner by allies. After Bourbon restoration created Marquis de Law, marshal and peer of France. {RGVIA, f.410; Zapiski A.P.Yermolova.M., 1991, pp.213, 236, 446}.

LAW [Лов] (+1709,Poltava). Colonel of dragoons. Most high-ranking Russian officer killed by Swedes at Poltava. Probably a Scot; mentioned by A.Gordon. {History of Peter the Great, I, p.301}.

LEARMONT(H) [Лермонт(ов)], GEORGE [Юрий Андреевич] (ca.1593-1634, near Smolensk). 1613 ensign, went over to Russians with other Scots in Polish garrison of Belaya. Served under Prince Pozharsky and granted land near Galich. Ruitmaster in war with Poles, killed at siege of Smolensk. His sons WILLIAM and HENRY [ANDREY] (+1652) were both ruitmasters, while PETER (+1679) became major, Orthodox convert and Governor of Saransk. 1688 Peter's sons YURY (+1708) and PETER (+1704) compiled a pedigree of their line, attested by P.Gordon, going back to reign of Malcolm III, King of Scots. They preserved their ancient coat of arms and added Russian ending "ov" to the name.

The Russian branch over eleven generations produced many outstanding figures in military and civil service, the greatest of them being the poet MIKHAIL YURYEVICH LERMONTOV (1814-1841). He had interest in Burns and Scott and expressed his yearning for Scotland in poems like "Tomb of Ossian" and "Desire". His relatives and acquaintances included Cobleys, Hamilton-Khomutovs, Mounseys and Barclays de Tolly. Strangely, he fell in a duel near a place called Little Scotland, founded by Scots missionaries in the Caucasus. L.'s earliest translation into English duly appeared in "Blackwood's Edinburgh Magazine", 1843, LIV. {Lermontovskaya Entsiklopediya}.

Ensign THOMAS L., seemingly unknown to Russian experts on the family, served in Muscovy under A.Leslie 1632 and could have fought at Smolensk alongside his namesake George. {RGADA, f.210, op.1, No.78}.

LEE [Ли], WILLIAM. Sub-ruitmaster in Leslie's regt. 1632.

ROBERT L. (1793, Galashiels-1877). Studied Edinburgh, M.D. 1814. 1824 engaged as personal physician by Count M.S.Vorontsov and arrived in Odessa via Kiev. Lived on Vorontsov's estates in Ukraine and Crimea and also practised widely using quinine against malaria, a novel measure in Russia. Visited Moscow and St.Petersburg and met J.Wylie. 1827 returned to Britain. Wrote "Last Days of Alexander I and First Days of Nicholas I, Emperors of Russia", L., 1854. {N.Shuster, "English Doctors in Russia", Procceedings of Royal Society of Medicine, LXI, 1968, No.2}.

LEISHMAN, PETER. Stonemason. 1784 came to Russia, aged 26, to work with C.Cameron. 1788 married Margaret Topping in St.Petersburg. {RBC, I; SSR, No.10, 1988}.

LENZIE [Лензи], JOHN. 1716 sub-lieutenant in Russian Navy. 1721 lieutenant, but resigned in a year. {OMS, I}.

LESLIE, or LESLY [Лесли], Sir ALEXANDER [Александр Ульянович, Авраам Ильич] (1590s?-1663, Smolensk). Also styled "of Auchintoul", the estate he held for some years. Russia's first General and reformer of Muscovite army. Son of William L. of Crichie of the Balquhain branch. 1618 officer in Polish employ, captured by Russians, but released. 1629 colonel in Sweden, sent by King Gustav Adolf on mission to Moscow and entered service of the Tsar. 1631 recruited thousands of soldiers in Western countries including Scotland and supervised first regiments "of foreign order", organised and armed along Western lines. 1632-4 one of Russian commanders in Smolensk War, went abroad after unhappy outcome of campaign. 1637 in Russia again, with recommendation from King Charles I, and finally settled in Muscovy 1647. 1652 embraced Orthodoxy with his family, richly rewarded and made general. 1654 wrested Smolensk from the Poles and became Tsar's Governor there. {RGADA, ff.35, 141, 150 & 210, op.1, No.78}.

His sons ALEXANDER [IVAN] (+1672) and FEDOR (+1691) were both colonels and left offspring. Genealogy of Russian Leslies compiled by S.V.Dumin, still incomplete and unpublished, lists 13 generations and 272 bearers of the name. Most men joined the army and fought in all Russian campaigns from Smolensk (1632-4) to World War II, including 7 generals, 8 colonels, 7 majors, 20 captains and 18 lieutenants, with another dozen in the Navy. {RGIA, f.1343, op.24, Nos.1738-44; Y.M.Lesli. Kratkaya istoriya blagorodnoy familii Lesli.Viaz'ma, 1893}.

Numerous clansmen of Gen.Leslie, not related to him directly, but some hired by himself, also appear in Russia. Lists of his regiment show Ruitmasters WILLIAM and PETER, Ensign "SIMS", Corporal "JENS", Drummer "JURGEN", Private WILLIAM and Capt. DAVID L. The latter also had testimonials from King Charles I as "commander in wars of France, Germany, Sweden and Low Countries". {PRO SP 91/2-212}.

Other Leslies in 17th-century Muscovy were: JOHN of Balquhain, cavalry colonel killed in storming castle of "Igolwitz" 1655; Capt.

ALEXANDER of Edenville (or Kininvie?- cf.Steuart,p.40), who died childless in Russia; JOHN (?) of Wardis, who returned to Scotland, and Col. JAMES of Aikenway, a warrior of great courage also known as "King of Love". {P.Dukes, "Aberdeen and North-East Scotland: Some Archival and Other Sources", The Study of Russian History from British Archival Sources, 1986, p.54}.

GEORGE L. Capuchin friar in Archangel, 17th century. {Steuart, p.40}.

GEORGE L. 1735 hired as lieutenant from Royal Navy. Took part in Turkish war 1735-9. 1740 arrested with W.Kenzie in Azov for refusing to obey Vice-Adm.Bredal. Tried at St.Petersburg and ordered out of Russia immediately, but still commanded a ship in 1743. {OMS, II, p.232}.

JOHN L. MELVILLE. Younger son of Earl of Leven and Melville. 1807 visited St.Petersburg which he described in letter to his brother, Viscount of Balgonie. {SRO, GD 26/13/861}.

LEWIS "OF MENAR" [Левис оф Менар]. Baltic noble family of Scots origin. Russian subjects from early 18th century. {RGIA, f.1343, op.24, Nos.1113-24 & op.51, No.600}.

LIDDELL, THOMAS. Died 5/7/1811, St.Petersburg, aged 32. {RBC, I}.

LINDSAY [Линдсай. Линдзей], THOMAS. Army captain from Leith who served in Britain, Holland and Venice. 1632 came to Moscow with recommendation to the Tsar and Patriarch Filaret from King Charles I, but was not accepted with the explanation that all officers' posts in regiments of "foreign order" were filled. {Phipps, pp.282-3, 296}.

JAMES L. 1680s mentioned by P.Gordon in Moscow and Kiev {Gordon, Diary}.

"IAN" L. Master blacksmith hired by Peter the Great in London 1698. Sent to Russia via Amsterdam and Narva {Ustrialov, III, pp.101, 581}. 1706 JOHN and SAMUEL L. founding members of British Congregation in Moscow. {RBC, I}.

JOHN L. Court painter to Empress Catherine II whom he accompanied on her Crimean journey 1787. {Steuart, p.124}.

LINDSAYS. Family stemming from Alexander L., officer ennobled by King of Poland 1764, whose offspring soon became Russian subjects.

They lived near Vilno and called their coat of arms "Balcarres" after the title of their clan chief. ANTON L. was sub-lieutenant in Murom Infantry Regt. 1843. {RGIA, f.1343, op.24, No.2019}.

LINGETT, JAMES (2nd half of 16th century). In the 1570s, during the Livonian War, Scots corps under Colonel Ruthven fought for Sweden against Russia. Some, at least 85 in number, were taken prisoner, brought to Moscow and entered Tsar's employ. Jamie L., "a valiant honest man", was appointed captain over his compatriots and led them in battles against Crimean Tatars. "Then had they pensions and lands allowed them to live upon, married and matched with the fair Livonian women, increased into families and lived in favor of the prince and people". {Rude and Barbarous Kingdom. L., 1968, pp.288-9}.

LIRIA Y BERWICK [Лирия и Бервик], JAMES STUART, Duke of (1695-1733, Naples). Eldest son of James Fitz-James, Duke of Berwick (1670-1734), natural son of King James VII (II), and a noted Jacobite. His father was created Duke of Liria in Spain. 1727-30 first Spanish ambassador in Russia where he became a Knight of St.Andrew. Ensured Russian employment for his friend J.Keith and met J.D.Bruce. Wrote well-informed memoirs, published in St.Petersburg 1845.
    Cf. Berwick and Stuart.

LISTER [Листер], THOMAS (1763-1832, St.Petersburg). Plasterer. 1784 went to Russia on invitation of C.Cameron, settled there and left a family. {SSR, No.10, 1988; RBC}.

LITTLE [Литтел(ь)], CHRISTIAN. 1632 served with A.Leslie's regt. in Muscovy. {RGADA, f.210, op.1, No.78}.
    ROBERT L. (+1735, Russia). Jacobite. 1717 entered Russian Navy as captain in Amsterdam. 1719 imprisoned for 6 months and demoted to sub-lt. for running his ship aground, but had rank restored 1722. His children were MARY (*1724) and PADON HENRY (bapt.Kronshtadt 1727). {J.Deane, History of the Russian Fleet during the Reign of Peter the Great. L., 1899; RBC, I; OMS, I}.
    ISAAC L. (1763-1821). Bricklayer. 1784 arrived in St.Petersburg to work under C.Cameron and remained in Russia. 1791 married Jean Lindsay and left a large family. {SSR, No.10, 1988, p.65; RBC}.

LIVINGSTON, JOHN. Merchant. 1630s member of Muscovy Co., though it is uncertain whether he actually went to Russia. {Phipps, p.449}.

ALEXANDER L. ,or Leviston [Левистон] (ca.1640-1696,Azov). 1666 captain in Pereyaslav infantry regt. 1668 gravely wounded by mutineers in Ukraine. 1680s colonel, served in Kiev under P.Gordon. 1684 signed petition to open first Catholic church in Russia. Took part in campaigns against Crimea and Azov where he was killed by a Turkish bullet. Lieutenant L. mentioned by Gordon was evidently his son, who became lt.-colonel by 1698. {P.Gordon, Diary; Ustrialov, II, pp.278, 285-6, 383}.

EDWARD L. died 10/3/1818, St.Petersburg, aged 41. {RBC, II}.

LOBANOV-ROSTOVSKY [Лобанов-Ростовский], Prince ALEXANDER YAKOVLEVICH (1788-1864). Fought in French wars, major-general. Passionate admirer of Mary Queen of Scots and collector of books, records etc. about her life. Published "Lettres et Memoires de Marie, Reine d'Ecosse", 7 vols., London, 1844. Bequeathed a 16th-century portrait of Mary to the Hermitage, St.Petersburg. {RBS; L.Arinstein, "Mary Stuart,Prince Lobanov-Rostovsky and Thomas Campbell", Notes & Queries, N.S., XX, 1973, No.3, pp.84-6}.

LOCKHART [Локкарт], ROBERT BRUCE (*1887, Anstruther, Fife). 1912 British Vice-Consul in Moscow. A popular figure in Russian society, he was also a good athlete and champion of Moscow Football League. Helped A.F.Steuart to write his book on Russo-Scottish ties. 1918 involved in so-called "Lockhart Conspiracy" in Petrograd, arrested by the Cheka and sent out of Soviet Russia. Wrote "Memoirs of a British Agent", L., 1932.

LODYZHENSKY [Лодыженский], Count I.N. Chief Commissioner of Russian Section at Glasgow International Exhibition 1901. Spent several months in Scotland with his daughter. {SSR, No.10, 1988, p.182}.

LOGAN [Логан], WILLIAM. Stonemason. 1784, aged 30, came to Russia on invitation of C.Cameron. 1788 married Jane Crawford in Tsarskoye Selo; their son JOHN born 1789. {SSR, No.10, 1988}.

ROBERT L. Master of ship "Roman Vassilievitch". Died and buried in St.Petersburg 1789, aged about 48. {RBC, I}.

LOVELL [Лавел], ARCHIBALD. Soldier in A.Gordon's company of A.Leslie's regt. Present at muster in Moscow 14/3/1632 and probably fought in Smolensk War. {RGADA, f.210, op.1, No.78}.

LUMSDEN, ALEXANDER (+1678, Chigirin). Possibly of the Pittullock family. Near kinsman of P.Gordon and officer (ensign?) in his regiment. Killed by Turks at Ukrainian fortress of Chigirin. {P.Gordon, Diary}.

THOMAS and Dr. MATTHEW L. Cousins from Aberdeenshire who travelled through southern Russia on their way from India to Scotland 1820. They went through Caucasus, Rostov, Taganrog, Nikolaev and Odessa. Thomas, lieutenant with Bengal Horse Artillery, described the trip in "A Journey from Merut in India to London", L., 1822.

LUNDIE [Лунди], D. Officer in Polish service. 1613 with other Scots who garrisoned the fortress Belaya surrendered and went over to Russians. 1632-4 took part in Smolensk war against Poland. {Stashevsky, Smolenskaya voyna}.

LUTKE [Литке], FIODOR PETROVICH (1797-1882). Russian naval officer of German descent, traveller and geographer. 1830, as captain of 1st rank, commanded a squadron of three frigates with Russian cadets who visited Scotland on their way to Iceland. 1847 accompanied Grand Duke Constantine on his Scottish tour and reported about it to Emperor Nicholas I. Later admiral, count and President of St.Petersburg Academy of Sciences. Founded and headed Russian Geographic Society. {RGAVMF, f.224, op.1, No.5; OMS}.

LYALL, LYLE [Лайелл]. Ensign PETER "LAYEL" enlisted to serve in Russia under A.Leslie, but was absent at muster in Moscow 14/3/1632. {RGADA, f.210, op.1, No.78}.

JOHN LYELL jr. from Kinnordy, Forfar, died in St.Petersburg 22/6/1797, aged 20. {RBC, I}.

ROBERT LYALL (1790, Paisley-1831). Doctor and botanist, graduate of Edinburgh. 1810s moved to Russia as physician to several noble families in Moscow. Travelled in different parts of the Empire. Returned to Britain to publish his well-illustrated book "The Character of the Russians and a Detailed History of Moscow", L., 1823, dedicated to Emperor Alexander I. His other work is "Travels in Russia, the Krimea, the Caucasus and Georgia", Edin. & L., 1825.

Cf. Semple Lisle

LYON [Лайон. Лион], PETER. Officer with A.Leslie's regiment in Muscovy 1632. {RGADA, f.210, op.1, No.78}.

WILLIAM L. (1732-1793x). Plasterer. 1784 sailed from Leith to Russia, aged 52, with his sons and assistants GEORGE, 20, and JAMES, 19, to work under C.Cameron. 1786 George (+1818, St.Petersburg) married Hellen Auld, and their daughter HELLEN was born 1788. James married his second wife, Mary Jarvis, 1808, and their son JAMES was born same year. {SSR, No.10, 1988; RBC}.

William's daughters also settled in Russia. JANE [Евгения Васильевна] (1771-1842) was appointed nurse to Grand Duke Nicholas by Empress Catherine 1796 and remained with the Imperial family until she died; her wards called her "nanny-lioness". 1805 she wedded Vasily Vecheslov. Her younger sister MARGARET married John Forman in St.Petersburg 1797.

MACALPINE [Макалпин], CHRISTIAN (1541,Wittenberg-1598, Denmark). Used Latin name Machabaeus. Son of Scots blackfriar and divine John M. and Agnes Matheson who settled in Denmark. Studied at Wittenberg, Copenhagen and Cambridge, then dean at Ely, professor at Copenhagen and canon of Lund Cathedral. 1568 and 1571 Danish ambassador to Muscovy. {T.Riis. Should Auld Acquaintance Be Forgot, I, pp.114-20; II, 68-9}.

GEORGE M. 1805-24 missionary at Scots colony of Karrass in the Caucasus.

JOHN M. (ca.1822-1901, Harrogate). 1847 married Catherine Wishart in St.Petersburg. JANET, ALEXANDER and ROBERT M. (their children?) died there 1854-5. {RBC, IV}.

MACCAUSLAND, ANDERSON. 1816 married Julia Forssmann in St.Petersburg and had issue. Still in Russia. 1823. {RBC, II}.

MACCORMICK [Маккормик]. American ambassador in Russia until March 1905 when transferred to France. {Dnevniki Nikolaya II, p.254}.

MACDANIEL, RICHARD. Died in St.Petersburg 12/11/1795, aged 54. {RBC, I}.

MACDONALD [Макдональд], John [Иван Александрович]. 1783 joined Russian Navy as midshipman. Served in Baltic fleet under S.Greig. 1784 lieutenant. 1788-90 fought against Swedes at Hogland, Krasnaya Gorka and Viborg, advanced to capt.-lt. 1797 resigned but apparently remained in St.Petersburg where his young wife died 1802. {OMS, IV, 299}.

ANN M. died in St.Petersburg 29/12/1801, aged 22. {RBC, I}.

JACQUES ETIENNE ALEXANDRE M. (1765-1840). Born Sedan of Scots father. One of Napoleon's best generals. 1799 his Italian corps was defeated at Trebbia by Russians ("My career was saved only because my victor was Suvorov", he said). 1809 made marshal and Duke of Tarente for his role at Wagram. 1812 commanded French corps in Courland, took Dunaburg and besieged Riga. 1814 persuaded Napoleon to sign his abdication and delivered it to Russian emperor.

HENRY CRAIGIE M. (1868-1909). Captain, 93rd Argyll and Sutherland Highlanders. Youngest son of an officer of 22nd regt. Commemorated on a tablet in British Church, St.Petersburg.

MACDONNELL. T(homas?) "Magdanil" officer in Tsar's army ca.1630. Evidently took part in Smolensk War 1632-4. {Stashevsky, Smolenskaya voyna}.
EVAN M. Lived in St.Petersburg by 1840. Witness at Murdoch Macpherson's wedding. {RBC, III}.

MACDOUGALL [Макдугал], PETER. 1880s Russian Vice-Consul in Leith and Edinburgh. {AK OR 1884}.

MACEWAN, DONALD. Possibly from Perth or Dundee. Jeweller in St.Petersburg by mid-18th century. A friend of the poet Allan Ramsay who wrote of him: "It is the mind that's not confin'd/ To passions mean and vile,/ That's never pin'd while thoughts refin'd/ Can gloomy cares beguile./ Then Donald may be e'en as gay/ On Russia's distant shore/ As on the Tay where usquebae/ He us'd to drink before". {Steuart, 114}.
JOHN M. Plasterer. 1784 came to Russia, aged 38, to work with C.Cameron. {SSR, No.10, 1988}.

MACFADYEN, ARCHIBALD (1790-1848,St.Petersburg). 1820 married Mary Frazer in Russian capital. Their sons were DAVID (*1821), ARCHIBALD (*1822) and WILLIAM (*1824). David also died in St.Petersburg 1843. {RBC}.

MACFARLANE, or MACFERLAIN, ELIZABETH (+1858, aged 84). Governess with the Counts Tolstoy and Zakrevsky. Mentioned by Dr.R.Wilson in his Russian diary. {King's College Library, Aberdeen}. Buried in Moscow.

MACGILL [Макгилль], T(HOMAS?). Wrote "Travels in Turkey, Italy and Russia during the years 1804, 1805 and 1806", Edin., 1808.
HUGH M. (1800, Scotland-1848, Moscow). 1840 married Isabella Muirhead in St.Petersburg.

ROBERT M. (1804, Carrickfergus-1887, Moscow). His wife was Jane Purdon (1804-1875) from Glasgow {Moskovsky nekropol', II, p.216}.

ROBERT M. (1824-1893, Moscow). Wealthy industrialist in Moscow, partner in "Wartze & McGill" Co. Owned iron foundry and textile mill. He and his wife Jane Hastie were benefactors of British Church of St.Andrew, Moscow. {H.Pitcher, The Smiths of Moscow}.

MACGOVAN. Name appears among parishioners of British Church of St.Andrew, Moscow, in late 19th and early 20th century. {H.Pitcher, The Smiths of Moscow}.

MACGREGOR [Макгрегор], JAMES. Moved to St.Petersburg by 1840. His son WILLIAM and daughter MARGARET MURRAY were baptized 1841 and 1844, and his wife Christina, nee Crichton, died there 1845. {RBC, III}.

JOHN M. (ca.1832-1872, St.Petersburg). Photographer. 1857 met W.Carrick in Edinburgh and joined him in Russian capital where they opened their photo studio 1859. Worked and lived with Carrick and died from a sudden illness. {Caledonian Phalanx, pp.93-100}.

MACKAY [Макай], "HANS" (JOHN?). Ca.1630 officer in Muscovite army. {Stashevsky, Smolenskaya voyna}.

ADAM "MAKEY". Private in R.Carmichael's company of A.Leslie's regiment. Present at muster in Moscow 1632 and probably fought at Smolensk. {RGADA, f.210, op.1, No.78}.

MACKENZIE [МакензибМекензи], GEORGE. Also M.-Quin. British minister in St.Petersburg from September 1714 to May 1715. {SRO, GD 24/1/449; Steuart, p.79}.

WILLIAM M. 1730s officer with Russian Imperial guards. 1740 received Russian passport to return home via Riga. {SRO, GD 46/6/ 97A}.

THOMAS [Фома Калинович (son of Colin)] (ca.1710-1766). 1736 hired as shipwright. Served in Kronshtadt, Archangel and Astrakhan. 1751 capt.-lt. Took part in Seven Years' War. 1764 rear admiral.

THOMAS [Фома Фомич] M. (ca.1745-1786, Sevastopol). Probably son of above. 1765 midshipman. 1769 lt. In action against Turks, commanded a fireship at Cesme which battle he described in "Scots Magazine". 1783 rear admiral, served in newly founded Black Sea Fleet and laid foundations of Sevastopol where local hills still bear his name. {OMS}.

Captain JAMES M. 1761 married Jane Benning in St.Petersburg. {RBC, I}.

MACKENZIE. 1820s prominent merchant in Archangel. 1828 present at foundation of new British church there, returned to Britain and delivered a letter from A.Izmaylov, writer and vice-governor of Archangel, to Sir Walter Scott. {Alexeyev, pp.361-3, 391}.

Cf. Kenzie.

MACKIBBIN [Маккибин], WILLIAM. Allegedly a sailor and a protestant. Settled in Russia in late 19th century. His three children belonged to hereditary nobility: WILLIAM [VASILY] (ca.1885-1930s) served under Bolsheviks, but was executed as "English spy". ELIZABETH MARY (1888, St.Petersburg-1983, Kharkov) studied in Moscow and married B.K.Viktorov. ALEXANDER (*ca.1890). Played football for "Union" club in Moscow, emigrated after 1917 and possibly acted as British agent in Estonia between World Wars. {Information from B.A.Viktorov, a descendant}.

MACKIE, FRANCIS MILTON (*1790). Lived for a time in Kinston-upon-Thames. In St.Petersburg by 1818, had many children by his wife Sophia, and still in Russia 1841. {RBC}.

MACKINNON, T(HOMAS?). 1630 "T.Miakinin, boyar's son from town of Tenriros", i.e. nobleman from Tain in Ross, arrived in Moscow via Pskov with other Scottish officers to serve the Tsar. Probably fought at Smolensk 1632-4. {Scot.Soldier Abroad, pp.50-1}.

CATRIONA M. (1778, Uisken,Mull-1858, Florence). Daughter of a blacksmith. 1804 left for St.Petersburg and became governess in aristocratic households and then in the Imperial family. Her ward was Alexander II whom she allegedly taught Gaelic. Ca.1847 went to Italy with a Russian princess. Her fortune was unsuccessfully claimed by relatives. Stories of her survive even today among Gaels in Mull. {Scot.Studies, XXXI, 1993, pp.88-100}.

MACKINTOSH [Макинтош], ALEXANDER (1749-1779, Petropavlovsk). Carpenter from Perth. Took part in James Cook's third expedition. Died when it anchored in Avachinsky Bay on Kamchatka coast.

MARGARET M. died 25/1/1823, St.Petersburg, aged 81. {RBC, II}.

MACLACHLAN. RICHARD MACLAUCHLIN (1762-1805) died and was buried in St.Petersburg. {RBC, I}.

MACLAREN, JOHN (1757-1799, St.Petersburg). 1787 married Diana "Dooar" in Russian capital. Judging by witnesses at the wedding he was associated with C.Cameron's men. His children were ELIZABETH ANN (*1789), MARGARET AMELIA (1791-1793), SOPHIA (1792-1815), WILLIAM (*1796) and JOSEPH (*1799).

Another JOHN M. married Margaret Macleroy in St.Petersburg 1809. Their son JOHN born 1811. {RBC}.

PETER M. (+1894, St.Petersburg). Engineer. 1864 became manager of M.Macpherson's Baltic shipyard in Russian capital. 1865 married Annie Norris from Govan and had 12 sons by 1885. Every three years the family spent summer in Scotland where the boys studied. JAMES (*1867), the eldest, 1889 went to Glasgow to master boiler-making and returned 1892. {F.MacLaren, "From Clyde to Neva", Scots Magazine, N.S., XLIII, No.4, 1945, pp.249-54}.

MACLEA, DUNCAN (1772-1827). Died and was buried in St.Petersburg. {RBC, II}.

MACLEAN [Маклин]. Private WILLIAM "MAKLEN" served in A.Leslie's regiment and company 1632. {RGADA, f.210, op.1, No.78}.

CHARLES M. 1798 married Anne Paterson in St.Petersburg and had offspring. {RBC}.

JOHN M. (1879, Glasgow-1923, ibid.). Socialist. Worked as schoolteacher. Condemned World War I, hailed Russian revolution and became Soviet Consul in Britain. 1918 convicted and spent some months in prison. 1920 took part in II Congress of Communist International in Petrograd and Moscow along with W.Gallacher and J.S.Clark. Ironically, St.Petersburg's English Prospekt was renamed after this Scot.

MACLELLAN. ROBERT "MACLILAN" appears as soldier in A.Leslie's regiment 1632 and probably fought at Smolensk. {RGADA, f.210, 0p.1, No.78}.

MACLEOD, JOHN. Master plasterer. From 1783 worked with C.Cameron at Tsarskoe Selo, notably on decoration of Great Palace and Cold Baths. 1787 was paid 850 roubles a year. Still in Russia 1798 {SSR, No.10, 1988; RBC, I}.

MACLEROY, JOHN. In St.Petersburg by 1806 when his son ALEXANDER (+1835) was born. WILLIAM M. (another son?) died there 1807, aged 10.
ALEXANDER M. (1840-1878), son of JOHN M. and Isabella McViccar who were married in St.Petersburg 1827, is buried in Vvedensky cemetery, Moscow, and other members of family appear in RBC.

MACLOTHLIN, RICHARD. Settled in St.Petersburg by 1798 when his daughter Amelia was born.
RICHARD WATSON M. (son of above?) and his family are recorded in Russian capital from 1820s to 1860s. {RBC}.

MACMICHAEL, WILLIAM. Wrote "Journey from Moscow to Constantinople", London, 1819.

MACMANUS [Макманус], ARTHUR (1889-1927). Leader of Clydeside shop stewards. 1920 founder and chairman of Communist Party of Great Britain. From 1921 member of Executive Committee of Communist International. By his will his remains lie in the wall of Moscow Kremlin.

MACMILLAN [Макмиллан], DANIEL. Died 25/2/1793, aged 35, in St.Petersburg.
Another DANIEL M. also died there 18/12/1799, aged 61. {RBC, I}.
ALEXANDER [Александр Карлович] M. British subject. 1840s lived in Moscow as trustee of Imperial Philanthropic Society. {Adres-Kalendar', Moscow, 1848}.

MACMURRICH, HUGH. Died 15/7/1800, aged 25, and buried in St.Petersburg. {RBC, I}.

MACNAB, WILLIAM. In St.Petersburg by 1816 when his daughter MARGARET (1815-1819) was baptized there. Her sister JANE born 1819. William M., Doctor of Medicine, (another?) died in Russian capital 1849, aged 55.

JOHN M. died 30/6/1833, St.Petersburg, aged 47.

THOMAS M. died there 2/3/1835, aged 45. He stayed some time with his wife Agnes at Sarepta on the Volga where their daughter MARGARET was born 1831. WILLIAM, his posthumous son, born 1835, St.Petersburg. {RBC}.

MACNAUGHTON, COLIN. Ruitmaster who served in Pskov. 1666 escorted P.Gordon from there to Swedish border. {Gordon, Diary}.

SALLY M. 1915 went to Russia to work in a field hospital. Wrote letters home. {SRO, GD 372/94}.

MACPHERSON [Макферсон], Donald. 1819-24 resided in Scots colony of Karrass in the Caucasus.

MURDOCH M. 1830s owned wharf on the Clyde. Built yachts on commission from Emperor Nicholas I who invited him to Russia 1839. 1841 married Julia Maxwell in St.Petersburg and supported a large family {RBC}. 1856 he established famous Baltic shipyard and foundry where Russia's first armored ships were constructed. Employed dozens of Scottish engineers and workers (no less then 70 families!) including Rob.Thomson and P.MacLaren. 1872 Baltic works became bankrupt and were taken over by the state, but the family survived, and one of them flirted with a promising Russian ballerina in late 1880s. {M.Kshesinskaya.Vospominaniya. Moscow, 1992, pp.20-1}.

Cf. Ferson.

MACQUIRE, JAMES. Recorded in St.Petersburg 1788 when his daughter CATHERINE was born. JANE, another daughter, died 1789, aged 15. A son, ROBERT, was born 1790.

JOHN JAMES, son of JOHN and Davida M. *1806, St.Petersburg. John died there 1819, aged 48. {RBC}. MARY (+1873,aged 68) and DAVIDA M. (+1840,aged 34) were buried in Moscow. {Moskovsky nekropol', II, p.216}.

MACSWINEY, Rev.J.H.H.   1850s British Chaplain in Kronshtadt. {RBC, IV}.

MACTAGGART [Мактагерт], IAN. 1783 enlisted in Russian Navy as midshipman. 1786 resigned. {OMS, IV, p.304}.

MACVAY, JAMES. Bricklayer. 1784, aged 37, came to St.Petersburg on invitation of C.Cameron. 1793 still employed by Russian Palace Office along with mason JOHN M. (his son or brother?). {SSR, No.10, 1988, p.64-5}.

MACVIC(C)AR, DANIEL (1771-1833, St.Petersburg). 1826 married Catherine Quinland, his second wife, in St.Petersburg. ISABELLA M. (probably his daughter) wedded JOHN MacLeroy 1827. {RBC}.

MAIN [Мейн], JAMES. 1650s colonel in Tsar's army, a Protestant. 1659 accused of perjury against a Moscow pastor, but pardoned. Evidently left issue: 1678 in 2nd Chigirin campaign Lt.-Col.YAKOV and cavalry major DAVID, sons of Yakov (James) M., figure in Burnett's regiment. Russian officers of that Scottish line served until 20th century. {Charykov, pp.354, 361; RGIA, f.1343, op.25, Nos.3042-3; H.Pitcher, Smiths of Moscow, p.74}.
GEORGE M. Stonemason. 1784, aged 25, came to Russia to work under C.Cameron. {SSR, No.10, 1988}.

MALINOVSKY [Малиновский]. See Russian.

MALLOCH. Doctor in St.Petersburg in mid-18th century. Mentioned by J.Cook in his "Voyages and Travels". {Steuart, p.114}.

MARR [Mapp], THOMAS. Soldier in A.Leslie's regt. 1632. {RGADA, f.210, op.1, No.78}.
JAMES [Яков Патрикиевич] M. (ca.1780-1874). 1822 settled in the Caucasus. After little luck in trade he succeeded in horticulture on estates of Prince Gurieli. Died aged nearly 95. By a Georgian he had a late son,

NIKOLAY (1864, Kutais-1934, Leningrad), noted linguist and orientalist. An Academician since 1912, he wrote on languages, history and ethnology of the Caucasus, founded and directed several scholarly and cultural institutes in Petrograd, but his "Japhetic theory", approved by Stalin and generally enforced, verged on insanity. {Vostok-Zapad. Moscow, 1988, pp.178-204}.

MATHESON [Матисон], GEORGE [>hbq]. Colonel in Russia from 1620s. Mentioned in Sir T.Urquhart's "Jewel". Active in Smolensk War 1632-4. His will is dated Moscow 1633; most of his belongings (clothes, arms, 7 books, carpet, mirror etc., and 300 roubles) were bequeathed to his kinsmen in Broughton near Edinburgh. {Scot.Soldier Abroad, pp.50-4}.
    EDWARD M. (+1720). Lieutenant in Russian Navy from 1715. {OMS, I}.

MAXWELL [Максвель], WILLIAM. 1632 mentioned in will of Capt.Wauchope whom he owed 3 roubles. As no military rank is given, he must have been a merchant or craftsman in Moscow. {Scot.Soldier Abroad, p.52}.
    JANE M. married Anthony Martin in St.Petersburg 1800.
    DAVID M. In St.Petersburg by 1834, had several children and died 1846, aged 43. JOHN M. died same year, aged 45. {RBC}.

MEADER [Мидер], JAMES. Gardener, designed park at Syon House for Duke of Northumberland. Wrote "The Planter's Guide, or Pleasure Gardener's Companion". 1779 came to Russia and laid out "English park" with cascade and grotto at Peterhof for Empress Catherine. 1783 lived in St.Petersburg with family of three. His watercolors are kept in the Hermitage.

MEIKLE, ARCHIBALD. Died 18/1/1841, aged 42, in St.Petersburg. {RBC, III}.

MELVILLE [Мелвиль], JOHN. Lutheran pastor in Courland, apparently of Scots descent. His son was Major-Gen. ROBERT HENRY (1837-1899x) who served in Siberia and Far East, became hereditary nobleman and had six sons by two wives, the second a GABRIELLE

MELVILLE. Had many relatives in Mitava and Libava. {RGIA, f.1343, op.36, No.15839}.

MENELAWS [Менелас], ADAM [Адам Адамович] (1749 or 1756, Edinburgh-1831, St.Petersburg). Architect. 1784 came to Russia on invitation of C.Cameron, but began a career of his own. Worked on churches in Torzhok and Mogilev and for Prince Razumovsky in Moscow and Ukraine, then employed by Imperial court. Moved from restrained classicism to exquisite neo-Gothic in his palaces and pavilions at Tsarskoe Selo and Peterhof. 1792 married Elizabeth Cave. {RGIA, ff. 266, 614, 637, 802, 1285, op.8, 1286, op.1; A.Cross, "In Cameron's Shadow: Adam Menelaws, Stonemason Turned Architect", SSR, No.17, 1991}.

Engineer-Colonel ALEXANDER M., obviously a relative, had a daughter, ELIZABETH (1833-1849, St.Petersburg). {Peterburgsky nekropol', III, p.97}.

MENTIETH, or MONTEITH [Мантифт], MICHAEL. 1652 was rewarded for conversion to Orthodoxy and "suffering imprisonment with the Turks". {RGADA, f.150, op.1, 1652, No.6}.

PETER "MANTET". Scots officer in Russian army in 17th century. {RIB, XXVIII}.

MENZIES [Менезийб Менезиусб Менезесб Менгес], THOMAS (+1660, Chudnov, Ukraine). Son of Alexander M. of Balgownie family. Served in Sweden as captain. 1654 came to Russia with J.Trail and promoted to lt.-col. Mortally wounded in battle with the Poles. His sons JOHN LEWIS (ca.1654-1691) and WILLIAM were born in Russia. John embraced Orthodoxy, served under D.W.Graham and P.Gordon, also rose to lt.-colonel and left issue.

PAUL [Павел Гаврилович] M. (1637, Maryculter near Aberdeen-1694, Moscow). 4th son of Sir Gilbert M. of Pitfodels. Studied at Douai. 1661 left Polish service with P.Gordon and enlisted in Tsar's army. 1672-3 Russian envoy to Germany, Austria and Italy, revealed great diplomatic skill, advanced to colonel and became first foreign tutor to young Tsarevich, future Peter the Great. Took part in Chigirin and Crimean campaigns. 1689 major-gen. A staunch Roman Catholic, he was involved in securing permission to open first church of his creed in Muscovy. His children by two marriages were THOMAS (1663-x1691), captain in father's regt., MAGNUS, captured by Swedes at Narva as major 1700, JOHN, ANDREW and CATHERINE. {P.Gordon, Diary; Charykov}.

DUNCAN M. In Russia by 1784. 1787 married Margaret Vassey in St.Petersburg. Associated with <u>C.Cameron</u>'s circle {RBC, I}.

MEYENDORF [Мейендорф], ALEXANDER KAZIMIRO VICH, Baron (1798-1865). Served in army, resigned as colonel. 1829 visited Scotland, stayed with Scott at Abbotsford and corresponded with him later: "Parmi les choses excellentes qui m'offrait Sir Walter et qui rappelaient tant ce que l'on sait de l'antique hospitalite ecossaise, je remarquai avec plaisir le whisky..." Then Russian minister in Berlin {Alexeyev, pp.349-54}.

Baron M. (his son?), of Russian Ministry of Finance, came to Scotland 1862 and visited Dundee. {RNL, MSS, f.806, No.8}.

MIDDLETON [Мидделтон], WILLIAM and JULIUS (brothers?). Officers in <u>A.Leslie</u>'s regiment 1632. {RGADA, f.210, op.1, No.78}.

MILLAR, MILLER [Миллер]. Lieutenant JAMES MILLAR present at muster of <u>Leslie</u>'s regiment in Moscow 1632. His salary was 12,5 roubles a month. {RGADA, f.210, op.1, No.78}.

JOHN M. Stonemason. 1784 sailed to Russia from Leith, aged 35, and worked with <u>C.Cameron</u> at Tsarskoye Selo. {SSR, No.10, 1988}.

Other Millers appear in RBC in 18-19th centuries, but their origin is uncertain.

MILNE, PETER. Managed foundries owned by <u>Demidovs</u> in the Urals and Siberia in mid-18th century. Mentioned in <u>J.Cook</u>'s "Voyages and Travels" {Steuart, p.114}.

MIRRIELEES [Мерилиз], ARCHIBALD (1797, Aberdeen-1877, near London). 1822 went to St.Petersburg on behalf of London house "Fisher & Co.". 1843 established his own business which became "<u>Muir</u> & Mirrielees", biggest department store in Russia. He married thrice and left a large family. 1857 left Russia with his third wife Jane Muir and entrusted his firm to her brother Andrew. {H.Pitcher, Muir and Mirrielees. Moscow, 1993}.

MITCHELL. 1680s lt.-colonel in Tsar's army {P.Gordon, Diary).

WILLIAM M. 1740s surgeon in Russia. His wife Mary was buried in St.Petersburg 1749, and others appear in RBC later.

WILLIAM M. married Elizabeth Roy in St.Petersburg 1805.

JOHN M. 1805-26 lived at Scots mission in Karrass in Northern Caucasus.

JAMES, son of JAMES and Elizabeth M., born St.Petersburg 1812.

ALEXANDER M. married Grace MacArthur, widow, 1834, and died in St.Petersburg 1838, aged 31.

MOFFAT [Мофет]. A Mr.M. appears in list of British residents in St.Petersburg 1782. {RBC, I}.

WALTER [Владимир Владимирович] M. (+1805). 1783 hired from British Navy as lieutenant. Took part in Swedish War 1788-90. 1801 captain of 2nd rank.

HAMILTON M. (+1819). 1788 midshipman, in action against Swedes. 1798-1800 in campaign against France. Awarded orders of St.Anne,3rd class, and St.George and St.Vladimir,4th class. 1818 captain of 1st rank.

SAMUEL [Самуил Иванович] M. (+1821). 1794 midshipman, sailed from Archangel to Kronstadt via Edinburgh. 1798-1800 in Dutch campaign against the French. 1805-7 in Mediterranean expedition. 1812 aide to A.Greig. 1821 captain of 1st rank. {OMS, IV, pp.403-6}.

There were other Russian officers of the name who became noblemen of Vitebsk region. {RGIA, f.1343, op.25, No.5945}.

MOIR, ETHEL. Member of Scottish Women's Hospitals during World War I. 1916 with her friend Lilias Grant via Liverpool, Archangel, Moscow and Odessa reached Balkan front and worked in Russian lines describing her experience. 1917 witnessed February Revolution in Petrograd before going home. {Scots in Russia, pp.84-95}.

MONTGOMERIE, ARCHIBALD. 1632 officer in A.Annan's company of Leslie's regiment in Muscovy. {RGADA, f.210, op.1, No.78}.

Major MONTGOMERIE. 1660s served in Tsar's forces. 1666 at a party in P.Gordon's house quarreled with the host and had a duel with him. {Gordon, Diary}.

MONYPENNY, MRS. (+1724, St.Petersburg). "A Scotch gentlewoman". Apparently a cousin of T.Gordon's wife whose first husband was William M. of Pitmilly. She had a son by Sir Henry Stirling, died soon after his birth and was buried in St.Alexander Nevsky monastery. {RBC, I; Steuart, p.86-7}.

MOODIE, ALEXANDER. Died 1/8/1827, aged 24, in St.Petersburg. {RBC, II}.

MORRISON, GEORGE. Mate in Russian Navy. 1725 married Mary Peterson, widow, in St.Petersburg. 1725-30 took part in Kamchatka expedition under Bering aboard "St.Gabriel".
GEORGE M. Servant to Lord Carysfort. Died 1785, St.Peterburg, aged 50.
CHARLES, son of WILLIAM and Mary M. born 1822, St.Petersburg. William died 1837, aged 55.
JAMES M. Died 21/1/1835, St.Petersburg, aged 45.
WILLIAM M. married Margaret Jones in Russian capital 1844. Their son WILLIAM born 1846; CHARLES and PETER M. were sponsors at his christening. The latter married Janet Waldie 1844. {RBC}.

MOUBRAY, JOHN. Officer in Muscovite army, 17th century. {RIB, XXVIII}.

MOUNSEY [Манзей], MICHAEL. Doctor. 1733 came to Russia with Prince Anton-Ulrich of Brunswick. 1740 court surgeon to infant Emperor Ivan Antonovich. His son LOGIN (Lewis?) (ca.1736-1801x) was state councillor and director of Vyshny Volochek canal system. His four sons served in the army, NIKOLAY (1784-1854x) becoming major-general, and the latter's son CONSTANTINE (1821-1899x) wrote a history of his regiment, Hussars of the Guard, and rose to full general. They were noblemen of Tver region. {RGIA, f.1343, op.25, No.1354 & op.36, No.15215}.
JAMES M. (1710, Skipmire, Dumfriesshire-1773, Rammerscales near Lochmaben). Evidently related to Michael. Studied at Edinburgh. 1736 in Russia as army doctor, made campaigns against Turkey and Sweden. Practised in Moscow, became court physician to Empress Elizabeth and privy councillor and head of Medical Chancellery under

Peter III. A keen naturalist, he introduced rhubarb to Britain. Married Joan, sister of J.Grieve. Returned to Scotland after the coup of 1762. {Caledonian Phalanx, pp.51-3, 57-8}.

MOWAT, RICHARD. Gardener employed by Elizabeth, "Duchess of Kingston". 1778 followed her to Russia and worked on her estate near Narva as well as for Empress Catherine until 1788. {A.Cross, Anglofiliya u trona, p.108}.

MARY, natural daughter of HENRY M. and Elizabeth Joyce, was born 1799 and baptized in St.Petersburg 1808. {RBC, I}.

MUIR [Мюр]. 1661 Lt. JOHN "MURIS" who served the Swedes joined his compatriot P.Gordon en route to Moscow and enlisted in Russian army. {Gordon, Diary}.

ROBERT M. Plasterer. 1784 came to Russia, aged 40, on invitation of C.Cameron with his wife Charlotte. Their daughter CATHERINE born in St.Petersburg 1785. Still employed by Russian Palace Office 1793. {SSR, No.10, 1988}.

HUNTER M. (+1805,St.Petersburg,aged 29). Married Elizabeth Fox 1800. Their children were MARY (1800-1801), WILLIAM (1801-1803) and ELIZABETH (*1804). {RBC}.

ANDREW M. (1817, Greenock-1899, London). 1852 arrived in St.Petersburg as partner of A.Mirrielees, whose wife was his sister JANE. 1857 became merchant of 1st guild and took over "Muir & Mirrielees". 1861 married Alison Philip,nee Bell, and had several children. 1874 returned to Britain, but revisited Russia. {H.Pitcher, Muir and Mirrielees. Moscow, 1993}.

MUIRHEAD, ANDREW. Married Margaret Kirkland in St.Petersburg 1809. Their children were WILLIAM (*1810), MARGARET (*1815), GILBERT (*1817) and ANDREW (*1819), last two born at "New Saratofka".

ANDREW, son of JAMES M. and Anne Burgess, born 1816; his sister MARY *1819. Others appear in RBC later.

MULLENDER, ISAAC. C.Cameron's master bricklayer. Arrived in St.Petersburg from Leith 1784, aged 45. {SSR, No.10, 1988}.

MUNRO [Мунро], DAVID. Died 12/2/1824, aged 45, in St.Petersburg.

GEORGE M. (+1850,aged 48). Ship-builder. 1838 married Maria Wetterbom in St.Petersburg. Their children: MARIA (*1838), MARGARET (*1841), DAVID (*1843), ANN (*1845), GEORGIANA (*+1846).

MURCHISON [МерчисонбМурчисон], Sir Roderick Impey (1792, Tarradale-1871). Geologist. Wrote "The Silurian System" 1838. 1840-1 in Russia under patronage of Nicholas I. Headed expedition to the Urals resulting in his definition of Permian period in "Geology of Europe and the Ural Mountains" (London, 1845). Received Russian orders of St.Stanislav and St.Anne. 1847 accompanied Grand Duke Constantine on his British tour. Founded chair of geology in Edinburgh. {RGAVMF, f.224, op.1, No.5}.

MURRAY [МурейбМуррай и дрю]. 1630 W(ILLIAM?) MURRAY accompanied A.Leslie from Sweden to Russia. {Stashevsky, Smolenskaya voyna}.

JAMES M. Captain in Muscovite army. 1632-4 took part in war with Poland. Signed promissory notes in camp near Smolensk 1633. {Caledonian Phalanx, p.12}.

ANDREW "MOREA", ETHAN "MOREY" and Lieutenant PETER "MORA" appear in Leslie's regiment 1632. {RGADA, f.210, op.1, No.78}.

WILLIAM M. 1821 married Agnes Gilbert in St.Petersburg. Their children: MARY (*1822), WILLIAM (*1825), JOHN (*1827), GRACE (1828), ROBERT BRUCE (*1830), DOUGLAS (*1831), WALTER SCOTT (*1832) and AGNES (*1834). {RBC}.

VLADIMIR VASILYEVICH M. Doctor. Died 1905, St.Petersburg. {Peterburgsky nekropol', III, p.186}.

NAPIER, GEORGE. 1730s-40s prominent merchant in St.Petersburg who traded with Persia. Connected with Sir H.Stirling, Admiral T.Gordon and other Jacobites. {SRO, GD 24/1/454 & GD 1/850/31-9}.

FRANCIS N. (1819-1898). 10th Lord N. and 1st Baron Ettrick. 1860-4 British ambassador to Russia. Later Governor of Madras.

NEILL [Нил], ALEXANDER. Captain from "Scottish land". Served in Muscovy. 1649 petitioned to leave for his homeland. {RGADA, f.150, op.1, 1649, No.3}.

NEPEYA [Непея], OSIP GRIGORYEVICH. Native of Vologda, merchant in Moscow. 1556 sailed with first Russian embassy to Britain aboard Richard Chancellor's ship which sank in a storm off Kinnaird Head near Fraserburgh. 7 of 16 members of his suite were drowned. According to the English (Hakluyt) his goods were "by the rude and ravenous people of the countrey thereunto adjoyning rifled, spoyled, and carried away". But Scots bishop Lesley says that N. "was weill intertenit be the cuntrymen, and conveyit thairfra to Edinburgh to the Quene regent, quha eftir guid intertenement causit Lord Hwme accumpanie him to Berwik". He spent over 3 months in Scotland and accomplished his mission in London. 1557 returned to Russia and disappeared from sight. {RGADA, f.35; J.Robertson, "Docs. relating to the first Russian Embassy in England", Archeological Journal, 1876, XIII, pp.71-80}.

NESBIT, ROBERT. 1730s lived in St.Petersburg with his wife Sarah. Their son GEORGE was baptized 2/10/1738, but died same day.

THOMAS N. Buried in St.Petersburg 17/12/1757 {RBC,I}.

NICHOLAS I [Николай Ш Павлович] (1796-1855). Russian Emperor from 1825. His nanny was E.Lyon. 1816, as Grand Duke, visited Scotland. His suite included Russian Scots, notably Dr.A.W.Crichton and Col.N.Mounsey. Received in Edinburgh by Lord Provost Arbuthnot and met Walter Scott who addressed an ode to him. Entertained at New Lanark by Owen. As Emperor favoured many Scots, i.e. J.Wylie, R.Murchison, W.Allan and the Bairds. {N.K.Shilder. Imperator Nikolay I. St.Petersburg, 1903}.

NICHOLAS II [Николай ШШ Александрович] (1868-1918). Last Russian Emperor 1894-1917. 1896 after coronation went on European tour including Scotland with his wife <u>ALEXANDRA</u> and infant daughter OLGA. Arrived in Leith and stayed with Queen Victoria at Balmoral where he went hunting. Wore uniform of Royal Scots Greys as their Colonel-in-Chief. {Dnevniki imperatora Nikolaya II. Moscow, 1991, pp.167-70}.

NICOL, WILLIAM. Blacksmith. 1772 married Margaret Shaw Ewing in St.Petersburg. Their children: WILLIAM (1773-1778), ANN LOUISA (*1776), MARGARET (*1778), CONSTANTINE (*1780), PRIMROSE (*+1784), WILLIAM (*1787). {RBC, I}.

NICOLSON [Николсон], Sir Arthur (1849-1928). 11th Bart. 1906-10 British ambassador to Russia. Firm supporter of Russo-British rapprochement. 1907 negotiated and signed bilateral Convention on Iran, Afghanistan and Tibet which sealed the Entente. Knight of St.Alexander Nevsky. 1916 created Baron Carnock. {DNB, 1922-1930, pp.637-9}.

NIVEN, JAMES. Blacksmith. 1784 came to Russia, aged 27, to work under <u>C.Cameron</u>. 1788 married Margaret Nicol in St.Petersburg. Sons born there: DAVID (*1789) and WILLIAM (*1795). {RBC,.I}.

OCHTERLONY [Охтерлони]. See Auchterlony.

OGILVIE [Огильви], GEORG BENEDICT, Baron (1644 or 1648-1710, Danzig). Great-grandson of James, Lord Airlie and son of George O. who became baron in Austria. Reached rank of field marshal. 1702 engaged for Russian service at 7,000 roubles a year. 1704 joined Peter the Great's army at siege of Narva and took the city. Reorganized and improved his troops. 1705 headed campaign in Lithuania and Poland. 1706 led Russian retreat from Grodno to Kiev, but resigned due to rivalry with Russian generals. Probably only man in history to hold supreme military rank for three different crowns (Austria, Russia and Poland-Saxony). {RGADA, ff.32, 96, 150; D.Bantysh-Kamensky, Biografii, I, pp.61-8}.

OGILVIE (+1737, near Azov). 1736 enlisted as lieutenant. During Russo-Turkish war commanded a vessel in Sea of Azov.

MICHAEL [Михаил Михайлович] O. (ca.1765-1805). 1783 midshipman, served in Black Sea. 1787-91 took part in Turkish war. 1798 sent to the Baltic. 1799 capt.of 2nd rank in Kronshtadt.

ALEXANDER [Александр Александрович] O. (1765-1847, St. Petersburg). Probably cousin of above. 1783 also enlisted as midshipman. 1788-90 in action against Swedes; 1799-1800 in Dutch expedition. 1803 capt. of 1st rank. 1811 became Russian subject. 1814 rear-admiral in Kronshtadt. 1824 vice-admiral. 1841 full admiral. Knight of St.Vladimir,4th class, St.Anne,1st class, and White Eagle. His descendants held lands in Tver region. His son ALEXANDER was also a naval officer, and grandson NIKOLAY was an engineer and directed Serebriansky works in the Urals. Name survives in Moscow today. {OMS; RGIA, f.1343, op.26, No.3142}.

OLENIN [Оленин], ALEXEY ALEXEYEVICH (1798-1854). Son of president of Academy of Arts,St.Petersburg. Served in army. 1825 resigned as captain. Involved in Decembrist movement, but avoided trial. 1825 in Scotland as guest of John Pringle, neighbour of Sir Walter Scott, whom he visited in Abbotsford and was presented with his portrait. Later entered civil service. Killed by his serfs. {Alexeyev, pp.262-4, 376}.

OLIPHANT [Олифант], THOMAS. 1851 married Ann Hay Christison in St.Petersburg. Some of Mirrielees family were among witnesses. {RBC, IV}.

ORLOV [Орлов], GRIGORY VLADIMIROVICH, Count (1778-1826). His father directed St.Petersburg Academy of Sciences. 1825 visited Edinburgh with his wife and met Alexander Young of Harburn, friend of Sir Walter Scott. Made arrangements for his nephew V.P.Davydov to study in Edinburgh. {Alexeyev, pp.221, 312, 813}.

ORRIE [Орри], ALEXANDER. Lieutenant on Russian service. 1632 present at muster in Moscow with Leslie's regt. and probably fought at Smolensk. {RGADA, f.210, op.1, No.78}.

PAISLEY, JAMES. Died 6/2/1806, aged 28, in St.Petersburg. {RBC, I}.

PAT(T)ERSON [Патерсон], ALEXANDER. Master plasterer. From 1783 worked with C.Cameron at Tsarskoe Selo. His daughter MARY born 1784, St.Petersburg. Mary P. married George Goodlet there 1810. {SSR, No.10, 1988}.
ALEXANDER P. (+1824x). Missionary. 1802 with H.Brunton founded Scottish colony in the Caucasus (Karrass). After mission closed he tried to keep it as his personal hereditary property. His son HENRY ALEXANDER (1812-1858x) was doctor in Russian navy and army and retired as aulic councillor 1852. He married a Russian and had two sons and two daughters in Piatigorsk, but failed to secure noble status since his rank was insufficient. {RGIA, f.1343, op.27, No. 1074}.
BENJAMIN PATERSEN (1748/50, Varberg, Sweden-1815, St.Petersburg). Painter and engraver, probably of Scots origin. 1787 settled in Russia. Famous for his views of Russian capital.
CHARLES P. Died in St.Petersburg 1/12/1806, aged 27. {RBC}.
JOHN P. (1776, Duntocher near Glasgow-1855). Member of British and Foreign Bible Society, worked in Scandinavia. 1812 moved to St.Petersburg with E.Henderson and established Russian Bible Society under Imerial patronage. Supervised printing and distribution of Society's works. 1819 persuaded London Missionary Society to send W.Swan and

R.Yuille to Selenginsk. 1827 left Russia. His second wife was Jane Greig. Wrote "The Book for Every Land: Reminiscences of Labour and Adventure in the Work of Bible Circulation... in Russia" (London, 1857). {Bawden. Shamans, Lamas and Evangelicals}.

WILLIAM P. (1800-1831, Alexandrovsky near St.Petersburg). 1826 married Mary MacVicar in St.Petersburg, fathered MARY (*1827), GRACE (*1829) and JAMES (*1831). Died of cholera.

PAUL [Поль], EDWARD and WILLIAM. Scottish officers in 17th-century Muscovy. {RIB, XXVIII}.

Rev.R.B.PAUL. 1836 travelled from Britain to Moscow and back and published "Journal of a Tour to Moscow" (London, 1836).

Cf. J.PAUL Jones.

PEEBLES, GEORGE. Scots officer in Tsar's army, 17th century. {RIB, XXVIII}.

PETROV [Петров], PIOTR (+1950s, London). Member of RSDWP. 1905 took part in Russian revolution. 1908 escaped from Siberian exile and settled in Glasgow with J.Maclean who taught him English. Later lived in Germany and London, but never in Soviet Russia. {Scots in Russia Exhibition at NLS, 1987}.

PHILIP(S) [Филип(с)], THOMAS. Scottish officer mentioned in 17th-century Russian pay registers. {RIB, XXVIII}.

WALTER [Владимир Василевич] PHILIP (1845, Port Elizabeth, S.Africa-1919, Moscow). Stepson of Andrew Muir whom he joined in St.Petersburg 1862. 1874 succeeded as head of "Muir & Mirrielees" and made it one of the leading commercial houses in Russia. 1883 married Laura Reid, a South African Scot. {H.Pitcher, Muir and Mirrielees. Moscow, 1993}.

PINKERTON [Пинкертон], ROBERT. Missionary. 1805 went from Edinburgh to Karrass, Scots colony in the Caucasus, and lived there for three years. Moved to Moscow as tutor in family of Prince Meshchersky. 1812 co-founder of Russian Bible Society and head of its Moscow branch. Published his "Extracts of Letters on His Late Tour in Russian Empire" (London, 1817) and "Russia, or Miscellaneous

Observations on the Past and Present State of that Country and its Inhabitants". (L., 1833).

ALEXANDER P. (1787-1829, St.Petersburg). In Russian capital with his wife Rebecca by 1821. Their sons: ALEXANDER (*1821), FREDERICK (*+1824).

THOMAS P. In St.Petersburg by 1829. 1835 married Ann Theakston, same day as ANN P. (sister?) wedded James Theakston, and had issue: ELIZABETH (*1836) and JOHN (*1838).

PISCHEKOV [Писчеков], DANIIL YAKOVLEVICH (1758-1825, near Belgorod). Priest's son who took up medicine and attended lectures at Edinburgh University from 1783. 1784 received M.D. from Aberdeen; his dissertation "De novo methodo psoram sanandi" was printed in Edinburgh and also appeared in Russia. 1785 P. returned home and worked as doctor in Roslavl' and Taganrog. Also interested in agriculture and botany. Translated J.Elliott's "Medical Pocket-Book" and issued other works. {IRLI, f.620, No.142; Cross, By the Banks, pp.140-5}.

POLETIKA [Полетика], PIOTR IVANOVICH (1778-1849). Diplomat and man of letters, of Greek ancestry. In winter 1813-4 stayed in Scotland with D.P.Severin and met Walter Scott who liked his name and his conversation. 1817 appointed Russian minister in USA, then senator. {Alexeyev, pp.254-5}.

POLLOCK [Поллок], WILLIAM. Died 9/7/1837, aged 62, and was buried in St.Petersburg. {RBC}.

POLOVTSOV [Половцов], ALEXANDR ALEXANDROVICH (1832-1909). Statesman and historian. Founder and chairman of Russian History Society, hon.member of St.Petersburg Academy of Sciences. From 1883 Russian Secretary of State. 1889 came to Scotland via Paris to stay with his friend "Berte" at "Balintor" castle, but hunting did not go well because grouse were hit by disease. 1890 negotiated agreement with Coats and other Scottish thread magnates whom he received in St.Petersburg. {A.A.Polovtsov. Dnevnik. Moscow, 1966}.

POLTORATSKY [Полторацкий], DMITRY MARKOVICH (1761-1818). 1783-4 visited Britain, attended lectures of Adam Ferguson and others at Edinburgh. 1792 acquired Avchurino estate near Kaluga and introduced various improvements using Scottish experience and machinery; it became one of the most advanced in Russia. Founded Moscow Society of Agriculture. {RNL, f.603, No.248; Cross, By the Banks, pp.89-90, 142, 285, 294}.

PORTER [Портер], WILLIAM. 1780s prominent merchant in St.Petersburg, partner in "P. & Browne". Corresponding member of Society of Antiquaries of Scotland. {RBC, I}.
Sir ROBERT KER P. (1777, Durham-1842, St.Petersburg). Spent childhood in Edinburgh, studied at Royal Academy in London. 1804 came to Russia as court painter. Travelled widely and produced portraits, landscapes etc. 1811 returned to Russia and wedded Princess Mary Scherbatov. Wrote "Travelling Sketches in Russia and Sweden" (London, 1809); "Narrative of the Campaign in Russia during the year 1812" (several edns.) and "Travels in Georgia, Persia, Armenia etc." (L., 1821-2). 1826-41 British Consul in Venezuela. Died on a visit to his daughter who married Russian officer Kikin. His sisters Jane and Anna were writers; the former's novel about William Wallace, "Scottish Chiefs" (1810), appeared in Russian, and she came to St.Petersburg herself. {RBC; Alexeyev, pp.158, 221, 251-5, 305, 389}.

POWELL, JOSEPH (ca.1735-1789, St.Petersburg). Engineer at Carron works. 1771 entered Russian service with A.Ramage. Worked in Lipetsk. 1778 his method of casting cannon attempted at Petrozavodsk was not a success, but he continued work at Izhorsky foundry. {RBC, I}.

PRESTON [Престон], JAMES (1738-1813, St.Petersburg). Served in Royal Navy. 1770 taken into Russian service by J.Elphinstone as capt.-lieutenant. In Mediterranean campaign until dismissed 1771. 1788 rejoined Russian navy as captain, awarded order of St.George, 4th class, for actions against Swedes. 1797 rear-admiral. 1799 retired. MARIA, wife of James P. (another?) died in St.Petersburg 1776, aged 32. {OMS, IV, pp.613-4; RBC}.

PRIMROSE [Примрос], ARCHIBALD. 1632 lieutenant in A.Leslie's regiment and company. Sergeant DAVID P. also present at muster in Moscow same year. Both probably fought in Smolensk War. {RGADA, f.210, op.1, No.78}.

PRINGLE. See Stoddart.

PROCTOR [Проктор]. Scot from Blairgowrie who lived in Archangel in early 20th century. {Information from Mrs.Eugenie Fraser}.

PURVIS, ROBERT (1759-1810, St.Petersburg). Stonemason. 1784 sailed from Leith to work with C.Cameron in Russia. His son DAVID born 1786, St.Petersburg, and his wife Margaret died there 1814. {RBC; SSR, No.10, 1988}.

RACHINSKY [Рачинский], STEPAN IVANOVICH (*1762). Studied at Naval Cadet Corps, St.Petersburg. 1774 corporal, accompanied J.Robison to Edinburgh together with N.Beliayev and I.Shishukov. Attended courses at University under Robison and Dugald Stewart. 1777 returned to Russia with Admiral S.Greig whose aide he became with rank of lieutenant. Freemason, orator of "Neptune" lodge in Kronshtadt. {OMS; Cross, By the Banks, pp.129-31}.

RAE, REAY [Рей]. WILLIAM RAE. "Captain of Scottish land". 1666 escorted P.Gordon from Moscow to Pskov. 1667 returned home with testimonials of his worth and loyalty from Tsar. {Gordon, Diary; NLS, Adv.Ch.A.130}.

JOSEPH REAY. 1799 married Harriet Hockaday in St.Petersburg. JOHN R. (Joseph's brother? they were each other's witnesses) wedded Mary Leitch 1801. Both had issue. Joseph died in Russian capital 1818, and John 1834, aged 64. {RBC}.

RAMAGE, ADAM (+1775, Lipetsk). Expert engineer with Carron works. 1771 he and J.Powell signed 6-year contracts to serve in Russia. Employed at Lipetsk cannon foundry {Caledonian Phalanx, p.29}.

RAMSAY [Рамзай], JAMES [Яков]. Silversmith to Tsar's court in Moscow. 1646 permitted to return home with his family. {RGADA, f.150, op.1, 1646, No.4}.

RICHARD [Юрий, i.e.George] R. (+1756, St.Petersburg). 1715 hired as shipwright with rank of captain. Worked at wharves of St.Petersburg and Kronshtadt. 1732 capt.-commodore. Margarita, wife of George R. (another?) died 1738. {OMS, I; RBC}.

Coat of arms of Finnish RAMSAYS, Russian subjects from 1809, is similar to Dalhousie family. General ANDREY EDUARD R. (1799-1877) was made baron 1856 and Russian commander-in-chief in Poland 1862. His son Gen.GEORGY EDUARD commanded Finnish corps from 1880. {RGIA, f.1343, op.28, No.581; RGVIA, f.484}.

JAMES R. (1771-1829, St.Petersburg). In Russian capital by 1817 when his son JAMES was born; ARTHUR followed 1819 and CATHERINE 1821. {RBC}.

Cf. Balmain.

RATTRAY, GEORGE. 1632 ensign with A.Leslie's regiment in Muscovy. Received 10 roubles a month. Probably took part in Smolensk campaign. {RGADA, f.210, op.1, No.78}.

RAZUMOVSKY [Разумовский], KIRILL ALEXEYEVICH, Count (1777-1829, Kharkov). Second son of Russia's Minister of Education. His standing and talents promised a brilliant career, but dissolute habits and mental illness interfered. Ca.1805 he visited Scotland for treatment, but never recovered. On return he was arrested, sent to a monastery in Suzdal and died in hospital. {M.Pyliayev. Staraya Moskva. Moscow, 1990, pp.232-5}. Counts Razumovsky had other Scottish connections, employing architects C.Cameron and A.Menelaws.

REDFERN [Редферн], WILLIAM. Scots officer in Muscovy mentioned in 17-century pay registers. {RIB, XXVIII}.

REID [Рид], GEORGE. 1690s captain in Russia. {P.Gordon, Diary}.
JOHN R. Stonemason. 1784, aged 22, came from Leith to St.Petersburg to assist C.Cameron. {SSR, No.10, 1988}.

RENNIE, RENNY [Ренни], GEORGE (+1794). Came from wealthy family of Montrose, who established trade in Riga in mid-18th century. His son was ROBERT [Роман Егорович] R. (1778, Riga-1832, St. Petersburg). Spent childhood in Montrose, then enlisted in Russian army. Fought against Poles and French. 1808 colonel. 1810 sent by Barclay de Tolly to Berlin as military agent. 1812 quartermaster of 3rd Army and major-gen. Won many decorations for bravery in battle and retired 1816. His daughter ALEXANDRA (1808-1873) married Gen. Count N.M.Lamsdorf. {RA, 1898, III, pp.413-6}.
ALEXANDER R. (+1827), merchant in Riga, was father of Major-Gen.GEORGE ALEXANDER (1825, Riga-1887, Bath) who studied at Montrose Academy and served in Bengal Horse Artillery.
J.RENNIE. Engineer at Carron works. 1774-7 helped A.Smith to install steam-powered water-pump in Kronshtadt docks.
A more famous colleague, JOHN R. (senior or junior?) visited St.Petersburg and Kronshtadt 1815. {NLS, MS 19822 & 19966; DNB, XVI; Caledonian Phalanx, pp.65, 68, 74}.

RIACH, REOCH [Peax], WILLIAM. Soldier in R.Carmichael's comany of A.Leslie's regiment. 14/3/1632 present at muster in Moscow. {RGADA, f.210, op.1, No.78}.

RICHARDSON [Ричардсон], WILLIAM (1743, Aberfoyle, Perthshire-1814, Glasgow). Son of a minister. 1768-72 in Russia as secretary to Lord Cathcart and tutor to his sons. Wrote popular "Anecdotes of the Russian Empire" (London, 1784). Later professor of Humanity at Glasgow known as poet and critic. {Alexeyev, pp.130, 175}.

RITCHIE [Ричи], LEITCH (1800-1865). Traveller and author. Published "Sir Walter Scott and Scotland" 1834. 1835 visited Russia and printed his illustrated "Journey to St.Petersburg and Moscow" (London, 1836). R. was esteemed by Russian writers O.Senkovsky and M.Zagoskin. {Alexeyev, pp.578, 605-7, 615-7, 640}.

ROBERTSON [Робертсон]. Several bearers of the name appear in A.Leslie's regiment 1632: Ruitmaster ARTHUR, Sub-Ruitmaster DAVID, Lt. JAMES, Ensign PETER, privates DAVID, THOMAS and two ROBERTS one of whom was ill. {RGADA, f.210, op.1, No.78}.
WILLIAM R. Sergeant in Austrian service. 1661 came to Moscow to seek temporary employment. {RGADA, f.150, op.1, 1661, No.1}.
JOHN R. (+1695, Azov). Skilled gunner and engineer, took part in first siege of Azov. Killed during a Turkish sally. {P.Gordon, Diary}.
DUNCAN R. (+1718). Son of Alexander of Struan. Colonel in Russia, "highly esteemed" by Peter the Great. Married a Robertson of Inches. Died in Sweden (as prisoner?). {Steuart, p.85}.
SAMUEL R. 1710-3 served in Russian navy. {OMS, I}.
DANIEL R. C.Cameron's stonemason. 1784 came to Russia from Leith, aged 36. 1785 married Christian Johnson. {RBC; SSR, No.10, 1988}.
CHRISTINA R. (1796-1854, St.Petersburg). Portrait and miniature painter. Possibly related to Scots artists Archibald and Andrew R. 1823-44 exhibited at Royal Academy, London. 1839 came to Russia and settled there 1844. Member of St.Petersburg Academy of arts. Her female models were mostly aristocracy and royalty. {Hermitage. Zapadnoevropeyskaya zhivopis'.Katalog, II, 1981, pp. 262-3}.
JAMES THOMSON, son of ROBERT R. and Jane Norrie, born

1845, St. Petersburg.
JOHN R. 1880s Russian Vice-Consul in Aberdeen. {AK OR, 1884}.

ROBISON [Робисон], JOHN (1739, Boghall, Stirlingshire-1805, Edinburgh). Studied and lectured at Glasgow. 1770 went to St.Petersburg as secretary to Adm.Knowles. Learned Russian and became Professor of mathematics and Chief Inspector of Naval Cadet Corps with rank of major. Tried to invite James Watt to Russia. 1774 returned to Scotland with cadets Beliayev, Rachinsky and Shishukov, and got chair of Natural Philosophy at Edinburgh. Hon. member of St.Petersburg Academy of Sciences. {DNB, XVII, pp.57-9; Cross, By the Banks, pp.129-30}.

ROGERS [Роджерс]. 1840s Scottish doctor who attended to British Embassy and colony in St.Petersburg. {H.Pitcher. Muir and Mirrielees, p.37}.

ROGERSON [Роджерсон], JOHN, of Dumcrieff (1741, Lochbrow- 1823, Wamphray, Dumfries). 1765 M.D., Edinburgh. 1766 came to Russia ending up court doctor and privy councillor. Keen naturalist; 1776 first Briton to become hon.member of St.Petersburg Academy of Sciences. 1783 co-founded Royal Soc. of Edinburgh. Empress Catherine gave him land in Belorussia and a collection of medals. 1816 retired to Scotland. His son also a doctor, but served in Britain.

His nephew WILLIAM (1761-1810, St.Petersburg) merchant in Russia from 1780s. Latter's successor was ALEXANDER R. 1832 he married Eliza Miller in Russian capital; their children were JOHN (*1832) and ELIZA. (*1835) {SRO, GD 1/620/1-32; NLS, Mss.3942; RBC; Caledonian Phalanx, pp.53-4}.

ROMANOV [Романов]. Russia's ruling dynasty. See Alexandra, Constantine, Nicholas I and Nicholas II.

ROSE, FRANCES (1640-1673x). Daughter of John R., possibly of Kilravock family, who died for the Stuart cause. Ca.1656 mother sent her with Col.John Gibson to Russia where she married a Briton and embraced Orthodoxy. Despite many petitions to Tsar she returned home only when a Polish officer abducted her 1673. {Phipps, pp.395-7}.

WILLIAM R. [Роэ]. 1783 midshipman. 1788-90 in action against Swedes; capt.-lt. 1798-1800 in Dutch campaign against Napoleon. 1807 capt. of 1st rank. 1810 capt.-commodore. From 1815 served in Kronshtadt. 1826 dismissed and deprived of rank for involvement with smugglers. {OMS, IV, pp.678-80}.

PAUL R. Died 8/2/1828 in St.Petersburg, aged 68.

ALEXANDER R. Died there 20/7/1843, aged 19. {RBC}.

ROSS [Pocc]. 1749 mate in Russian navy; sub-lt. in Archangel. 1752 nearly demoted for loss of ship, but acquitted. Served until 1757 as lt. between St.Petersburg and Danzig transporting wines for Russian Court. {OMS, II, pp.356-7}.

ROSS. From ca.1780 wealthy merchant in St.Petersburg. His partner was a Mr.Warre.

ROBERT R. M.D. 1819-25 doctor at Karrass, Scottish colony in the Caucasus.

THOMAS R. Died in Russian capital 1823, aged 22, FRANCIS R. +1834, aged 62, and another THOMAS +1843, aged 77. {RBC}.

ROUTLEDGE, JOHN. C.Cameron's bricklayer. 1784 arrived in St.Petersburg aged 29. 1787 married Mary Craig. {RBC; SSR, No.10, 1988}.

ROWAND, JAMES. Obviously related to William R. of Bellyhouston for they matriculated similar arms together in Lyon Register. 1770s merchant in Moscow. 1780 helped S.Desnitsky to publish his agricultural treatise "Nastavnik zemledelchesky". {Lyon Reg., I, p.411; Cross, By the Banks, p.82}.

ROXBURGH [Роксбург], WILLIAM [Василий Василевич]. Relative of S.Greig from Inverkeithing. 1764 enlisted in Russian navy as capt. of 2nd rank. 1766 capt.of 1st rank. 1770-5 in Mediterranean expedition against Turks, fought at Chesme and awarded cross of St.George, 4th class. Promoted to rear-admiral, but retired to Scotland 1777. {OMS, IV, p.682 & V, 443}.

ROY, PETER. Master of the ship "Patriot" of Montrose. Died 2/8/1844 and was buried in St.Petersburg. {RBC, III}.

"RUSSIAN" [Россиянин]. Anonymous visitor to Scotland who spent 4 months there, mostly in Edinburgh, 1790-1 and published his impressions in Moscow 1796. It is arguably the best Russian account of 18th-century Britain. A.G.Cross suggested that it was VASILY FEDOROVICH MALINOVSKY (1765-1814), noted diplomat and man of letters. {"Priyatnoe i poleznoe preprovozhdenie vremeni", Nos.IX-XI, 1796; Cross, By the Banks, pp.32-3, 143-4}.

RUTHERFORD [Рутерфорд], ROBERT. Of Fairnington. 4th son of Sir John R. of that Ilk. Merchant in Leghorn. 1770s Russian agent in Tuscany. 1777 granted Barony of Russian Empire and coat of arms by Catherine II. Died unmarried. {NLS, Acc.7676/A/Bdl.38; Steuart, pp.123-4}.

RUTHVEN [Ровен], DAVID. Scots officer in Russian army, 17th century. {RIB, XXVIII}.

SABAKIN [Сабакин], LEV FEDOROVICH (1746, Staritsa-1813, Izhevsk). Self-taught mechanic. 1784 sent to Britain, studied English and mathematics in London. 1786 stayed in Edinburgh with M.Terekhovsky, met J.Robison, J.Black and J.Watt and visited Carron works. On return to Russia published "Lectures on mechanics, hydraulics and hydrostatics" based on J.Ferguson's work. Revisited Britain with his son (below) and was employed in the Urals under A.F.Deriabin.

IVAN LVOVICH S. (+1802, Birmingham). Studied under his father with whom he came to London 1797. 1799-1801 attended lectures on physics and chemistry by Robison and T.Hope in Edinburgh. Died of tuberculosis en route home. {F.N.Zagorsky. Lev Sabakin, mekhanik XVIII v., 1963; Cross, By the Banks, pp.189, 194-203}.

SA(U)NDERS [Сандерс], ANTHONY. 1632 sub-ruitmaster in A.Leslie's regiment where an IAN S. also served. {RGADA, f.210, op.1, No.78}.

WILLIAM HENRY [Андрей Осипович] S. Colonel of sappers in Russia. Published his "Poetical Translations from the Russian Language", London, 1826.

SAUNDERS. Aulic councillor under Alexander I. {Steuart, p.135}.

SAWERS, COLIN CAMPBELL (1797-1848, St.Petersburg). Married Margery Forman in St.Petersburg 1823. Their children: MARGARET (*1826), JOHN (*1828), ALEXANDRA MARY OLGA (*1829), WILLIAM (1832-1834), NICHOLAS (1833-1835), COLIN CAMPBELL (*1837), EDMUND (*1840), ALFRED and ALICE (*1845). {RBC}.

SCHOLTS [Шольц_], GHERMAN ALEXANDROVICH (1881-1928, Archangel). Came from russified German family of timber and flax merchants who had partners in Scotland. 1903 went to Dundee on business. 1905 married Helen Cameron in Broughty Ferry and took her to Archangel where their children EUGENIE and GHERMAN were born. Both families exchanged frequent visits. {E.Fraser. The House by the Dvina. Edin., 1984}.

SCOTT [Скотт,Шкот], JAMES. 1613 quit Polish service for that of Russia with other Scots officers. Probably fought in Smolensk

War 1632-4. {RIB, XXVIII}.

Colonel GEORGE S. [Юрий Андреевич Шкот], mentioned by P.Gordon 1680s-90s, started a distinguished noble line in Russia. His son ANDREY was also colonel, grandson ANDREY major-gen., and the latter's grandson PAVEL YAKOVLEVICH (1815-1880) vice-admiral. {RGIA, f.1343, op.33, No.2007}.

SCOTT-PISTOHLKORS [Пистольккорс]. Noble family of Scottish origin in Sweden and Russia {H.von Pistohlkors-Forbushof. Schottische Familien in Finnland und Schweden. Baltische Monatschr., LXVII, 1909}.

BENJAMIN S. senior (+1751, St.Petersburg). Maker of mathematical instruments. His son BENJAMIN jr. settled in Russian capital by 1748 and became master at the Imperial Mint. 1761 left Russia with his family. {A.Sivers, "Medal'er B.Scott", Izvestiya GAIMK, V, 1927, pp.157-78}.

WILLIAM S. (+1767, St.Petersburg). 1762 married Catharine Loscheat and had issue.

WALTER S. died in St.Petersburg 5/11/1778, aged about 30, and many others appear later; over 20 of them figure in RBC, vol.I alone (before 1812).

STEVEN [Степан Григорьевич] S. (ca.1760-1813). 1783 lieutenant in Baltic Fleet. In action against Sweden 1788-90 and France 1798-1800. 1807 capt.-commodore in Kronshtadt. {OMS, V, pp.84-5}.

JAMES HERCULES S. (1782-1848) was buried in Moscow with his wife Jessie Duncanson. {Moskovsky nekropol', III, pp.112, 359}.

ALEXANDER [Александр Яковлевич] S. (ca.1799-1860/1). Managed estates of Naryshkin and Perovsky families in Penza region. Head of agricultural firm "S. & Wilkins". Married A.P.Alferyeva, aunt of the writer N.S.Leskov who worked under S., described him in his stories and called his two sons "shkotiata" (Scotties). {A.Leskov. Zhizn' N.Leskova, I, Moscow, 1984}.

SCOTT. British ambassador to Russia until 1904. See Dalkeith.

SCOUGALL, GEORGE (+1826, St.Petersburg, aged 70). In Russia by 1782. 1797 married Catherine Mudrich and fathered HENRY (*1797), MARY ANN (*1798) and ALEXANDER (*1799). {RBC}.

SCRYMGEOUR [Скримгер и др.], WILLIAM. 1632 ruitmaster in A.Leslie's regiment where a JAMES S. also figured.

LAWRENCE S. 1650s colonel whose regiment stood in Smolensk. {RGADA, f.210, op.1, No.78 & f.141, op.3, No.23}.

SELKIRK, JAMES. 1720s-30s surgeon in Russian Imperial Guards. 1726 married Mary Bernard in St.Petersburg. Acquainted with J.Cook. {RBC, I; Steuart, p.114}.

LORD S. visited Russia under Catherine II {Caledonian Phalanx, 38}. Title belonged to Douglas Hamiltons; it was probably Thomas, 5th Earl of S. (1771-1820).

SEMPLE LISLE, JAMES GEORGE (1750, Irvine-1799x). Soldier and adventurer. 1779 went to Russia and enlisted captain in the army. Became aide to Prince Potemkin and major. 1784 fled the country leaving huge debts. Imprisoned in London, he wrote "The Life of Major J.G.Semple Lisle" (1799) in answer to the expose "Memoirs of Major S.,Northern Imposter and Prince of Swindlers" (London, 1786). JAMES S. (+1785, St.Petersburg, aged 3) was probably his abandoned son.

SETON, Lord CHARLES, 2nd Earl of Dunfermline (1608-1673). Known in Russia as "Lord Erhart", i.e. Urquhart, one of his titles. Leading Covenanter and royalist. 20/1/1659 signed 3-year contract as "generalissimo" of Tsar's forces, but soon departed. After Restoration Lord Privy Seal. {RGADA, f.150, 1659, No.3; DNB, XVII, pp. 1203-4}.

SEVERIN [Северин], DMITRY PETROVICH (1792-1865). Diplomat and author. 1813-4 visited Scotland with P.I.Poletika and met Walter Scott whom he regarded as "first among living English poets". Described his impressions praising Scottish achievements in philosophy. Later Russian minister to Switzerland. {"Rossiysky Muzeum", 1815, I, No.3, pp.270-5; Alexeyev, pp.254-5, 374, 377}.

SHA(I)RP [Шарп], PETER. 1661 came to Muscovy to serve as ensign. {RGADA, f.150, op.1, 1661, No.13}.

Lt.-Col. ANDREY VILIMOV and Ruitmaster ALEXANDER VILIMOV (i.e. sons of William) S., obviously brothers, took part in 2nd Chigirin campaign 1678. Alexander fought in Crimea and Azov and became major-general during Great Northern War. {P.Gordon, Diary; Ustrialov}.

WALTER SHAIRP (1720/1-1787, St.Petersburg). Son of Thomas S. of Houston. Merchant in Russian capital by 1752 when he married Eleonora Lindeman. British Consul General there from 1776. His children: STEPHEN (Consul General in Russia 1796-1807), MARGARET (1753-1754), JANET (bp.1755), THOMAS (bp.1756). ALEXANDER S. (+1815, aged 45) was warden of British church in St.Petersburg. {RBC}.

SHAND, ALEXANDER (bp.1770, St.Petersburg). Natural son of ALEXANDER S. and Helen Galloway.

WILLIAM AITKIN CARMICHAEL S. 1851 married Emily Cummings in Russian capital. {RBC}.

SHAW [Шав,Шоу], JAMES. Ruitmaster. 1613 one of 32 Scots in Polish garrison of Belaya fortress who enlisted in Russian army. Fought against Poles 1615 and 1632-4 and rewarded with land and money. {RGADA, f.150, op.1, 1615, No.2}.

ANDREY S. 1615 officer in Tsar's army.

JOHN S. 1632 sergeant in D.Leslie's company of A.Leslie's regiment. {RGADA, f.210, op.1, No.78}.

JAMES S. Died 7/10/1833 in St.Petersburg, aged 50.

JOHN S. 1841 married Matilda Leigh in Russian capital. {RBC}.

SHEKHTEL [Шехтель], FIODOR OSIPOVICH (1859, Saratov-1926, Moscow). Russian architect of German ancestry. 1900-1 spent several months in Scotland building pavilions for Russian section of Glasgow International Exhibition; they were constructed of wood by 200 Russian carpenters. S. considered them as his greatest creation and won diploma as best architect of the show. {C.Cooke, "Shekhtel in Kelvingrove and Mackintosh on the Petrovka", SSR, No.10, 1988}.

SHESHKOVSKY [Шешковский], IVAN STEPANOVICH (1763-1818). Son of head of Russian "Secret Expedition". 1777-9 lived in Edinburgh with the Dashkovs, but led dissolute life neglecting studies at university and ending up in prison for debts. {Cross, By the Banks, pp.134-6}.

SHIPLAW [Сипуля,Сапульоу и др.]. Rare Scots name after a place near Peebles, terribly distorted in Poland and Russia. JOHN S. (+1921, Kharkov), a Roman Catholic, was stonemason in Russian Poland and Ukraine. He had five daughters and two sons including EDWARD-WALDEMAR (WALTER?) S. (1892, Warsaw-1961, Ulyanovsk), engineer and World War I veteran who joined Communist Party, but stressed his Scottish nationality even then. {G.F.Black, Surnames of Scotland, p.723; Information from A.E.Karabanov-S.}.

SHISHUKOV [Шишуков], IVAN NIKOLAYEVICH (ca.1760-1811x). Entered Naval Cadet Corps in St.Petersburg. 1774 went to Edinburgh with N.Beliayev and S.Rachinsky to study at university under J.Robison. 1777 returned to Russia to teach English at Naval Corps. 1808-11 produced incomplete Russian-English dictionary. Secretary of masonic lodge "Neptune". {Cross, By the Banks, pp.129-31}.

SIMPSON [Сим(п)сон], "SANDER". 1632 ruitmaster in A.Leslie's regiment where privates CHRISTOPHER and IAN S. were also on record. {RGADA, f.210, op.1, No.78}.

Officers ALLAN and JOHN S. appear in 17th-century Russian pay registers. {RIB, XXVIII}.

HENRY [Андрей] S. From 1703 in Russian navy as capt. of 1st rank. Served until 1715 in the Baltic, Black Sea and Archangel. {OMS, I}.

ROBERT S. (1748-1822, St.Petersburg). M.D. 1774 invited to Russia by S.Greig and served on his ship. 1792-4 chief doctor at Military Hospital,Kronshtadt, then practised privately and had an imposing funerary monument "from 25 grateful families". Left a large family, including CHARLES (1795-1824, St.Petersburg), also a doctor. {RBC}.

JOHN S. Stonemason. 1784, aged 28, arrived in Russia from Leith to work with C.Cameron. {SSR, No.10, 1988}.

SINCLAIR [Синклер], MALCOLM (1691-1739). Ensign of Swedish Guards. 1709 captured by Russians after battle of Poltava; in confinement until 1722. 1737 major, sent on secret mission to Turkey. His murder by Russian agents was a pretext for Russo-Swedish war 1741-3. {S.M.Soloviev, X-XI}.

Sir JOHN S. of Ulbster, Bart. (1754-1835). M.P. 1786 made a tour through Riga, St.Petersburg, Moscow and Kiev. Wrote "General Observations Regarding the Present State of the Russian Empire", 1787. Hon. member of Russian Free Economic Society. President of Board of Agriculture; initiated "Statistical Account of Scotland". {Alexeyev, pp.143, 180, 353-4}.

MALCOLM S. Lived in St.Petersburg from ca.1790. His children: HUGH (1791-1793), JAMES (*1793), MALCOLM (1795-1839), ALISON (*1797), GEORGE (*1798). ANNE, daughter of George, (1846-1897) married Prof.V.V.Dokuchayev, eminent geologist. {RBC}.

SKENE, GEORGE. 1617 officer in Muscovite army. {Phipps, p.459}.

JAMES "SHENE" died in St.Petersburg 10/9/1789, aged 50. {RBC, I}.

SLATER, ANDREW (+1786). Blacksmith. 1784, aged 24, sailed from Leith to St.Petersburg to work with C.Cameron, but died shortly. {SSR, No.10, 1988}.

SMIRNOVE [Смирнов], CONSTANTINE YAKOVLEVICH (ca.1780-1843). Son of Orthodox priest of Russian Embassy in London. Died in Scotland and was buried at Duddingston near Edinburgh. His anglicized relatives probably visited Scotland too, and his two sisters certainly did. {Cross, By the Banks, pp.44-52}.

SMITH [Смит]. Origins of bearers of the name are not easy to trace, but some Russian Smiths definitely sprang from Scotland. Several are recorded in A.Leslie's regiment 1632. {RGADA, f.210, op.1, No.78}.

1661 Captain SMITH quit Swedish service with his wife and joined his compatriot P.Gordon en route to Moscow. {Gordon, Diary}.

JAMES S. Merchant in London and Archangel. 1731 made his will preserved in SRO in Edinburgh.

ADAM S. Namesake and contemporary of great economist. Chief engineer at Carron works. 1774-7 headed team of Scots who installed steam-powered water pump in Kronshtadt docks. 1783 he was joined in Russia by his son ALEXANDER who designed a "fire machine" of his own 1792. {RBC; Caledonian Phalanx, pp.28-9, 65}.

Doctor JAMES S. died 12/8/1832 in St.Petersburg, aged 30. {RBC}.

CHARLES PIAZZI SMYTH (1819, Naples-1900). Astronomer Royal in Scotland and pioneer photographer who introduced magnesium flash. 1859 made a tour of St.Petersburg, Novgorod and Moscow taking over 100 shots with his camera. Wrote "Three Cities in Russia" (London, 1862). {Alexeyev, pp.234, 243}.

RICHARD [Родион] S. (1824, Glasgow-1902, Moscow). 1847 invited to Russia to help in railroad construction. 1856 established his boiler works in Moscow. Married Janet Millar. 1916 their grandson HARRY sold the factory and departed after revolution. A Moscow street was named after them. {H.Pitcher. The Smiths of Moscow. Cromer, 1984}.

SOLOVIEV [Соловьёв], VLADIMIR SERGEYEVICH (1853-1900). Philosopher and poet, son of famous historian. 1893 came to Scotland staying at Inversnaid on Loch Lomond where he translated part of Scott's "Lady of the Lake". He observed that "Gaelic is closer to Russian than to English" and later tried to find a mystical affinity, based on "Scottish second sight", between M.Lermontov and his legendary forebear Thomas the Rhymer. {S.M.Soloviev. Zhizn' i tvorcheskaya evoliutsiya V.Solovieva. Brussels, 1977, p.318-9}.

SOMERVILLE HEAD, Sir ROBERT POLLOCK, Bart. 1915 married Grace Margaret Robertson in Petrograd. {SRO, GD 374/78}.

SPENS, SPENCE [Спенс], JAMES. 1620s appears in Muscovy {according to Dr.Graeme Herd}.

Lt.-Col. SPENS of Swedish service taken prisoner at Poltava 1709 and spent some years in Russia. {Zhurnal ili podennaya zapiska Petra Velikago, I, p.202}.

DAVID S. (ca.1750-1782,near Kerch). 1771 signed as lieutenant from Royal Navy. Served in Mediterranean under S.Greig against Turks. 1777 capt.-lt. 1781 sent to Taganrog, but soon drowned off Crimean coast. {OMS, V, p.115}.

STARK [Старк]. 1668 Lt.-Col. STARK was engaged in building "Orel", Russia's first warship, at Dedinovo on Oka river. {RGADA,f.150,op.1,1668,No.30a}. YAKOV IVANOV (James, son of John) S., ensign in Cooper's regiment, took part in 2nd Chigirin campaign

1678. {Charykov, p.361}.

NIKOLAY S. (+1845) was capt.of the guards, but many served in the navy including rear-admirals OSCAR VIKTOROVICH, after whom a strait near Vladivistok is named, and GEORGY KARLOVICH S. (+1950, Paris). Their scions live in Russia today, particularly in Yaroslavl. {OMS; Peterburgsky nekropol", IV, p.156}.

STEEDMAN, LAWRENCE. Stonemason. 1784, aged 36, sailed from Leith with other Scottish craftsmen to work with C.Cameron. Apparently left Russia 1790. {SSR, No.10, 1988}.

STEELE [стил], JAMES. Scots officer mentioned in 17th-century Russian pay registers. {RIB, XXVIII}.
ELIZABETH S. died 1815, aged 60, in St.Petersburg. JOHN S., widower, married Elizabeth Norman there 1816 and died 1827, aged 75. {RBC, II}.

STEPANOV [Степанов], MIKHAIL STEPANOVICH. Secretary of Russian Admiralty College. 1786 studied mathematics at Edinburgh University and became member of Natural History Society. Mediated with success in Russian government's bid to sign C.Gascoigne. {AKV, XIX, pp.374-6, 391-4}.

STEVENSON [Стивенсон]. ROBERT "STENSON" was a Scot in Russian army, 17th century. {RIB, XXVIII}.
JANNET S. died in St.Petersburg 1835, aged 53. ALEXANDER S. (+1843, St.Petersburg, aged 56), widower, married Elizabeth Manners 1836 and fathered JOHN (*1837), LUCY EUPHEMIA (*1839) and ALEXANDER (*1841). {RBC, III}

STEWART, STUART [Стюарт,Штуарт], WILLIAM. 1610s-30s officer in Tsar's army. {RIB, XXVIII}.
ALEXANDER S. Captain employed in Britain and Denmark. 1631 came to Moscow with recommendation from Charles I, but not accepted by Tsar. Also failed as agent of "Muscovy Co." and retaliated by seizing some of its ships. {Phipps, pp.131-2, 261, 269, 295-6}.
GILES S. Officer in A.Leslie's regiment 1632. {RGADA, f.210, op.1,

No.78}.

JAMES S. (+1671). 1647 hired in Holland and despite his poor show at a muster came to Russia as captain and rose to lt.-colonel. 1671 his widow Magdalen and children were allowed to go home. {RGADA, f.150, op.1, 1671, No.7; Soloviev, V, p.593}.

ROBERT S. 1661 left Swedish army for that of Russia with other Scots on advice of P.Gordon and enlisted in D.Crawford's regiment. {Gordon, Diary}.

ALBERT [Альбрехт Томасов] S. 1678 ensign in P.Menzies' regt. during 2nd Chigirin campaign. 1683 capt.-lt., demanded by D.W.Graham for his regt. {Charykov, pp.353, 428, 430, 438-9, 589-90}. 1690s lt.-col. S. (same?) mentioned by P.Gordon.

STUARTS. 1703 created barons of Sweden. Russian subjects after conquest of Livonia 1710. Bar.FRIEDRICH-GUSTAV [Федор Федорович] S. (1804, Libava-1856, St.Petersburg) was actual state councillor and translator from Greek. His sons DMITRY (1838-1902) and ALEXANDER were confirmed Barons of Russia 1893; former was privy councillor and director of State Archives in St.Petersburg. {RGIA, f.1343, op. 46, Nos.2094-2100}.

PETER S. (+1756,St.Petersburg). In Russia by 1724. Married Margaret, "a Finnswoman", and fathered ELIZABETH (bp.1724) and MARY (bp.1726).

NEILL S. was buried in St.Petersburg 1739 and dozens of his namesakes appear in RBC later.

STUART. Grenadier officer (colonel?). Served under J.Keith in Finland during Russo-Swedish war 1741-3. {RNL, MSS, Avt.136, No.49}.

STUART-HALIBURTON. Noblemen of Poland and Grodno region of Russian Empire. Andrew S.-H. left Scotland ca.1660. His grandson ANTHONY S.-H. (1751-1829x) served in Russia from 1771 and left issue. Their coat of arms was called "Morton". Several other STUARTS were also ennobled in Russia. {RGIA, f.1343, op.29, Nos.7510-13}.

WILLIAM S. (+1775). 1771 signed from Royal Navy as lieutenant. Took part in Mediterranean campaign against Turks. 1773 capt.-lt. {OMS, V, p.139}.

1784 among C.Cameron's workmen there were stonemasons CHARLES, aged 37, and JOHN, 23, and blacksmith CHARLES S., 27. Former was dismissed 1786, but others continued work at Tsaskoe Selo.

Charles jr. died in St.Petersburg 1813. {SSR, No.10, 1988}.

STUART. 1830s-40s owned a restaurant in Kronshtadt. {P.V.Annenkov. Parizhskie pis'ma. Moscow, 1983, pp.234, 557}.

CHARLES, Baron S. de ROTHESAY (1779-1845). Grandson of Earl of Bute, British prime minister. 1841-4 British ambassador in St.Petersburg.

Cf. Berwick and Liria.

STIRLING [Стирлинг], PAUL. Born Danzig of Scots parents. 1589 captured by Russians in Livonia. On release became interpreter to the Tsar. 1615-6 assigned to Dutch envoys who commended his skill and conduct. Still served 1630s. {Proezzhaya po Moskovii. Moscow, 1991, pp.236-7, 259, 266, 268}.

WALTER S. Officer in A.Leslie's regiment 1632. {RGADA, f.210, op.1, No.78}.

Sir HENRY S., 3rd Bart. of Ardoch (1688-1753). Nephew of R.Erskine. 1717-41 Jacobite agent in Russia. By Mrs.Monypenny had a natural son, CHARLES (1724-5). 1726 maried Anne, daughter of Adm.T.Gordon in St.Petersburg where their sons WILLIAM (ca.1730-1799) and THOMAS (1733-1808), commander of Black Watch in America, were born. {Hist. MSS Commission. Calendar of Stuart Papers. London, 1902-23}.

STODDART [Стоддарт], WILLIAM PRINGLE [Василий Фомич]. 1786 midshipman. 1787 lt. 1788-90 fought in Russo-Swedish war. Resigned by 1792. {OMS, V, p.130}.

STRACHAN [Страхан], JOHN and WILLIAM (brothers?). 1632 ruitmasters in A.Leslie's regiment where another WILLIAM S. is also recorded. {RGADA, f.210, op.1, No.78}.

STRANACK, JOHN. Shipmaster and merchant. 1770s-80s traded in Kronshtadt and St.Petersburg. Member of "Neptune" masonic lodge headed by S.Greig. SARAH S. 1801 married Andrew Duncan in St.Petersburg. {RBC}.

STRATHERN, GEORGE. Died 27/2/1823, aged 52, and buried in St.Petersburg. {RBC, II}.

SUTHERLAND [Сутерланд], ALEXANDER (+1721). 1719 enlisted in Russian navy as lieutenant. {OMS, I}.

Brothers ALEXANDER (+1760) and JOHN S. (+1757) came to Russia from Holland as shipwrights 1736. Built large warships in St.Petersburg, Kronshtadt and Archangel and rose to colonel and major respectively. Alexander's sons were RICHARD (1739-1791), JOHN, a merchant (1742-1773), GEORGE (1745-1793) and ALEXANDER (bp.1753). Richard became court banker to Empress Catherine, state councillor and Baron of Russia 1788, but went bankrupt and committed suicide. His children were SARAH (bp.1766) who married John Browne in St.Petersburg 1788, and RICHARD (1772-1825, St. Petersburg) with whom baronial line ended. {RBC; OMS; A.Cross, "Sutherland Affair and its Aftermath", SEER, I, No.117, 1972, pp.257-75}.

Cf. Duffus.

SWAN [Сван,Шван], ALEXANDER. Ensign, present at muster of A.Leslie's regiment in Moscow 1632. {RGADA, f.210, op.1, No.78}.

Rev.WILLIAM S. (1791, Milltown of Balgonie, Fife-1866, Edinburgh). 1818 with R.Yuille established Christian mission at Selenginsk near Lake Baikal. Produced first translation of Bible into Mongolian. Married Hannah Cullen who followed him to Siberia. 1841 left Russia after mission closed. Wrote the poem "Idolatry" (Glasgow, 1827) and "Letters on Missions" (London, 1843). Later Secretary of Scottish Congregational Union and editor of its magazine. {Bawden, Shamans, Lamas and Evangelicals; Alexeyev, pp.598, 601, 648-9}.

SWINTON, ANDREW. 1788 came to Russia to see his kinsman Adm.S.Greig and stayed there until 1791. Wrote "Travels into Norway, Denmark and Russia" (London, 1792), published in several countries. {Alexeyev, pp.128-9, 173-5}.

TATLOCK, ROBERT. Art critic. 1916 leader and secretary of Quaker relief mission for Russian refugees in Buzuluk, Samara region. Visited German front and witnessed revolution in Petrograd and Moscow. 1918 returned to Britain. {R.C.Scott. Quakers in Russia. L., 1964}.

TEREKHOVSKY [Тереховский], MARTYN MATVEYEVICH (1740-1796). Native of Ukraine. Studied in Kiev and Strasburg (M.D.). 1786 spent some months in Edinburgh with L.F.Sabakin. Elected hon. member of Medical and Natural History Societies. {AKV, XII-XIII; Cross, By the Banks, pp.138-9, 195}.

THOMSON [Томсон], WILLIAM. 1632 corporal in A.Leslie's regiment where a PETER T. also enlisted. Both served in companies commanded by Scots officers. {RGADA, f.210, op.1, No.78}.

1784 plasterer JAMES, aged 27, and stonemason WILLIAM T., 22, arrived in Russia from Leith to work with C.Cameron at Tsarskoe Selo. Former absconded to Scotland 1786. {SSR, No.10, 1988}.

DAVID T. (1809, Glasgow-1872x). Worked as mechanic in Liverpool. 1845 moved to Russia to become chief engineer of Postal Fleet. Stayed in Britain during Crimean War, but returned as engineer on steamship "Vladimir". His son ROBERT became chief engineer at M.Macpherson's Baltic works in St.Petersburg and then manager for Wohrmann Co. in Riga 1870s. {Scots Magazine, N.S., XLIII, No.4, 1945, pp.249-54}.

Cf. Famintsyn.

TIRRELL, JOHN. Scots officer recorded in 17th-century Russian pay registers. {RIB, XXVIII}.

TODD, JOHN. Stonemason. 1784, aged 32, came to St. Petersburg with other Scots to work under C.Cameron. {SSR, No.10, 1988}.

TOPPING. Family of bricklayers who came to Russia from Leith to assist C.Cameron 1784. They were WILLIAM, aged 41, THOMAS, 35, MARK, 29, and JOSEPH, 25, all married. William's "Russian" children were CAMERON FORRESTER (*1784) and THOMAS (*1787) while THOMAS fathered FRANCES (*1785), ANN (*1787) and

ELIZABETH (*1790). MARGARET T. married P.Leishman in St.Petersburg 1788. All must have left for home 1790. {RBC, I; SSR, No.10, 1988}.

TRAIL [Трайл], JOHN. Captain "from Scottish land". 1654 came to Moscow from Sweden to serve Tsar with T.Menzies. {RGADA, f.150, op.1, 1654, No.1; Charykov, pp.76-7}.

TRETYAKOV [Третьяков], IVAN ANDREYEVICH (1735-1776). Son of army officer from Tver. 1761-7 studied at Glasgow University with S.Desnitsky under A.Smith, T.Reid, J.Black and J.Millar. Graduated M.A. and Dr. of Laws. On return lectured on law and expounded Smith's theory in Moscow. 1773 retired. {N.Taylor, "Adam Smith's First Russian Disciple", SEER, XLV, 1967, pp.424-38}.

TROTTER [Троттер], HENRY, Esq. Buried in St.Petersburg 9/1/1763. {RBC, I}.

TURGENEV [Тургенев]. Three famous members of this family made it to Scotland. NIKOLAY IVANOVICH T. (1789-1871). An official at Ministry of Finance, he took part in secret Decembrist movement against Russian autocracy, but was away during rising of 1825. 1826 proceeded to Scotland where he learned he was wanted for trial, and decided to stay abroad. Visited Aberdeen and Glasgow. Later moved to France and was pardoned 1856. {Dekabrist N.I. Turgenev. Pis'ma k bratu S.I.Turgenevu. Moscow, 1936}.
ALEXANDER IVANOVICH T. (1784-1845). Traveller and author. Secretary of Russian Bible Society. 1828 followed his brother Nikolay to Britain, stayed with Scott at Abbotsford, visited Melrose, Edinburgh and Glasgow, met Zachary Macaulay, publisher John Murray, Francis Jeffrey, Lords Minto and Rosebery et al. He kept detailed record of his impressions and bought a copy of P.Gordon's diary. {IRLI, f.309; A.I.Turgenev.Khronika russkogo. Dnevniki. Moscow, 1964; Alexeyev, chapter 5}.
IVAN SERGEYEVICH T. (1818-1883). Celebrated novelist. 1871 came to Edinburgh to deliver a speech at W.Scott's centennial. Stayed for a week with friends at "Allean House" in Pitlochry hunting grouse. He admired Burns as "clear fountain of poetry". Turgenev's first English

translator was the Scot J.D.Meiklejohn ("A Hunter's Notes", 1855). {I.S.Turgenev. Polnoe sobranie sochineniy i pisem. Pis'ma, IX, 1965; The Scotsman 10/8/1871; SSR, No.2}.

TURNBULL. Family established in Russian capital by 1825 when MARY T. witnessed a wedding. BENJAMIN T. (1784-1853,St. Petersburg) married Henrietta Rohdendorff 1835. Their children: MARY (*1836), WILLIAM (*1839), HENRIETTA (*1841) and PETER ALEXANDER (*1844). {RBC}.

UR(R)IE [Урий], JOHN. Colonel. 1647 came to Moscow with other Scots to seek employment, but sent abroad several months later. Probably related or even identical with Sir John U. (Hurry) of Pitfichie in Aberdeenshire who fought in British Civil War. {RGADA, f.150, op.1, 1647, No.27; D.Dorward. Scottish Surnames, 1995, p.341}.

URQUHART [Урварт, Уфорт, Оргерт, Архворт и др.], EDWARD. 1632 served in A.Leslie's regiment in Muscovy. {RGADA, f.210, op.1, No.78}.
ADAM U. 1650 enlisted in Tsar's army as captain and was rewarded. Ca. 1670 applied to British government to help him leave Russian service with his family. {RGADA, f.150, op.1, 1650, No.8 & 1651, No.16; PRO, SP 29/281A}.
ADAM U. (+1719). 1718 joined Russian Navy as lieutenant, took part in campaign against Swedes. 1719 capt.-lt. Killed trying to save his ship which ran aground. {OMS, I, pp.23, 380; J.Deane. History of Russian Fleet during Reign of Peter the Great. L., 1899, p.71}.
Cf. Seton.

VAN DER VLIET [Фан-дер-Флит], NIKOLAY FIODOROVICH (1840-1896). Of Netherlandish ancestry. Official of Russian Ministry of Finance. 1862 went to Britain to prepare an industrial exhibition. Travelled to Edinburgh where he admired the Castle, University, Industrial Museum and Heriot School. Visited Dundee, Perth,

Trossachs, Oban, Iona and Glasgow and wrote diary. Later rose to actual state councillor. {RNL, MSS f.806, Nos.8-9}.

VIGOR [Вигор], NORTH (+1769, St.Petersburg). 1747 M.D., Edinburgh. Practised in Russia and became court doctor. 1755 received certficate of his worth from Empress Elizabeth (in Library of Royal College of Physicians, Edin.) and returned home, but regained his post under Catherine II. {RBC, I}.

WALKER [Вакар,Валкер], D. Ca. 1630 enlisted in Tsar's army. 1632-4 active in Smolensk War. {Stashevsky, Smolenskaya voyna, p.34}.

GEORGE W. Captain-commodore. One of first officers of Russian Navy, senior in rank of 10 Scots hired in Amsterdam by Tsar Peter's "Great Embassy" 1698. Came to Moscow via Archangel and was recommended to P.Gordon. His pay was 40 thalers a month. {Gordon, Diary; Ustrialov, III, p.576-7}.

DAVID W. C.Cameron's bricklayer. 1784, aged 40, sailed from Leith to work in Russia. {SSR, No.10, 1988}.

THOMAS W. M.D. Farmer's son from Polmont, Stirlingshire. 1820-30s practised in St.Petersburg. 1829 matriculated his arms in Lyon Office, with "Scottish fir eradicate proper" for crest. {Lyon Reg., III, 69; RBC}.

WALLACE [Валлас,Уоллес], HENRY. 1632 drummer in A.Leslie's regiment and company. {RGADA, f.210, op.1, No.78}.

PETER W. 1755 cadet at Naval Corps,St.Petersburg. 1766 sent to Britain as lieutenant, but absconded by 1770. {OMS,.II}.

JAMES W. died in St.Petersburg 1828, aged 73, and ELIZABETH W. +1831, aged 78 (his widow?). Another ELIZABETH W. died there 1849, aged 48; "Ms. Wallace" was "dame de classe" at Catherine's Institute for girls in St.Petersburg 1820s. {RBC; A.O.Smirnova-Rosset. Dnevnik.Vospominaniya. Moscow, 1989, pp.155-6, 306-7, 344, 498}.

DONALD MACKENZIE W. (1841, Boghead, Dumbarton-1919). Writer and journalist. 1870 invited to Russia and got interested in "zemstvo" form of administration which he observed in Novgorod region. On return published his popular "Russia" (London,1877, 1905 & 1912).

Often revisited the country later and attended coronation of <u>Nicholas II</u> whom he accompanied on Asian tour 1890-1. Became director of "The Times'" Foreign Department and advisor to British government. Also wrote "Our Russian Ally", 1914. {Dnevniki Nikolaya II, pp.326, 342, 358}.

WARDLAW [Вардла,Вардвлав], JAMES. Major in <u>A.Leslie</u>'s regiment 1632. Probably left Muscovy after Smolensk War. 1636 Scottish lt.-col. James W. appeared in Moscow, but was not employed. 1645-6 colonel of that name successfully applied for a post in Tsar's army. {RGADA, f.150, op.1 & f.210, op.1, No.78}.

WATSON [Ватсон], ROBERT. 1632 ruitmaster in <u>A.Leslie</u>'s regiment and company. {RGADA, f.210, op.1, No.78}.
ANDREW W. Master plasterer. 1784, aged 27, came from Leith to St.Petersburg to assist <u>C.Cameron</u>, but returned home 1786. {SSR, No.10, 1988}.

WAUCHOP [Вахоб], JAMES. Captain. 1630 came to Russia from Sweden with <u>A.Leslie</u>. 1632 fell ill and made a will in Moscow, where he wished to be buried, in favour of his wife Ellen Cragg and son Colin, with Col.<u>Matheson</u> as executor. His belongings included 145 roubles, 10 gold ducats, some jewelry, a Scots cloak and 3 barrels of "aquavytey". {Scot. Soldier Abroad, pp.50-2}.

WEMYSS [Виммес и др.], JAMES. Colonel, probably related to <u>A.Leslie</u>. Served in Holland and Sweden for 19 years. 1629 came to Russia his with wife, servants and two Scots officers. Received money, goods and 500 serfs from Tsar. 1632-4 fought in Smolensk war. {Stashevsky, Smolenskaya voyna}.

WHITEFORD, WALTER. 1660s colonel in Muscovy. Ca. 1663 petitioned British government to help him leave Russia for fear that "eternal slavery" could befall his family if he deserted. {P.Gordon, Diary; PRO SP 29/74-73}.

WILKIE, WILLIAM (1768-1822, St.Petersburg). 1806 married widow Margaret Carrick (+1811,aged 42) in Russian capital. They had a daughter, MARGARET (*1807). {RBC}.

WILLIAMSON, "HANS" (JOHN). Scots officer in Russian army, 17th century. {RIB, XXVIII}.

ROBERT W. 1834 married Frances Cumming in St.Petersburg. Their children: ALEXANDER (1835-1837), ROBERT (*1837), IDA (*1838), MARY OLIPHANT (*1840), WILLIAM (*1841), GEORGE (*1843), FANNY (*1845). {RBC, III}.

WILLISON [Вил(л)исон], DUNCAN [Данило Иванович]. 1736 hired as shipwright. Served in Archangel and Kronshtadt. 1751 capt.-lt. Took part in Seven Years' War. Nearly fired for drunkenness, but advanced to capt. of 1st rank 1763. Resigned 1764. {OMS, II, pp.74-5}.

ELIZABETH W. Died and was buried in St.Petersburg 1783, aged 20. {RBC, I}.

WILSON [Вильсон], JAMES (1749-1821). Master smith from Edinburgh. 1784 came to Russia with his wife Helen and children: ALEXANDER, LUKE, CHRISTINE and JOHN; then came twins HELEN and MARIAN (*1785) and JAMES (*1787). He was highest paid of C.Cameron's workmen at 900 roubles a year and employed at Sestroretsk foundry under C.Gascoigne from 1790. James' eldest son ALEXANDER [Александр Иванович] (1776-1866), became Russian subject, engineer-general, director of Alexandrovsk textile mill in St.Petersburg and Izhorsky iron works in Kolpino. His brother John (*1783) was partner in St.Petersburg merchant house of T.Bonar, while James was mintmaster at Kolpino works. {RGIA, f.1343, op.18, Nos.2274-6; RNL, MSS f.536; RBC; SSR, No.10, 1988}.

WILLIAM RAE W. (1772, Paisley-1849, London). Traveller and author. Studied law at Glasgow. After a trip to St.Petersburg published 2-volume "Travels in Russia", London, 1828. {DNB, XXI, p.621; Caledonian Phalanx, pp.69-70}.

ROBERT W. (1787-1870). Surgeon and traveller. Graduate of Marischal College, Aberdeen. 1840s toured St.Petersburg and Moscow. Stayed with Wylies. Left diary. {MS in King's College Library, Aberdeen}.

WILLIAM SHARPE W. (1863, Old Deer-1935, Riga). Graduate of Aberdeen. 1892 went to Russia as private tutor and became one of best lecturers of English there. Taught at major institutions in the capital including Naval Corps, University (professor 1905), Alexandrovsky School of Engineers and Mikhailovsky Artillery Academy. Founder and chairman of St.Petersburg Guild of Teachers of English. 1920 arrested by Bolsheviks, then moved to Riga. {University of Aberdeen. Records of the Arts Class 1880-4. Aberdeen, 1922, p.120-1}

WINRAM [Винрам], JAMES. Lt.-colonel in Russia from 1662. 1663 married Juliana Keith in Moscow. {P.Gordon, Diary}.

WOOD [Вуд], JOHN and ANDREW (brothers?) were among Scots in Polish service who surrendered and joined Russians at Belaya fortress 1613. 1632-4 fought against Poles at Smolensk, and later Russian Woods must have stemmed from them. {Stashevsky, Smolenskaya voyna; RIB, XXVIII}. 1628 Ruitmaster JAMES W. served in "Great Regiment" in Tula. {Soloviev, V, p.267}.

Soldiers IAN and JOB W. enlisted in A.Leslie's regiment and company 1632. {RGADA, f.210, op.1, No.78}.

Captain IAN W. came to Moscow to serve Tsar with Col.Urie and others 1647. {RGADA, f.150, op.1, 1647, No.27}.

JOHN [Иван Александрович] W. 1678 ruitmaster in same regt. as J.Chambers. Missed Chigirin campaign because of illness. {Charykov, p.357}.

PAUL W. 1697 page in Tsar Peter's "Great Embassy" to Western Europe. {Ustrialov, III, pp.7, 572}.

WYLIE [Вил(л)ие], Sir JAMES [Яков Васильевич], Bart. (1768, Kincardine-on-Forth- 1854, St.Petersburg). Younger son of a farmer. Studied medicine at Edinburgh. From 1790 surgeon in Russia. Court doctor to three Emperors, W. rose to actual privy councillor, Chief Medical Inspector of the Army, president of Medico-Chirurgical Academy of St.Petersburg and Russia's only baronet. Published first works on surgery in Russian and founded "Military Medical Journal". Bequeathed most of his fortune for establishment of Mikhailovsky Clinic of Bart.Wylie in St.Petersburg. Died unmarried, but many of his kinsmen came or moved to Russia. {RGVIA, ff.26, 316, 879; RNL, f.145; Caledonian Phalanx, pp.60-4}.

Dr. JAMES [Яков Васильевич] W. Jr. (1795-1850, St.Petersburg).

Nephew and colleague of above. From 1817 in Russia, physician to Grand Duke Mikhail. His brother GEORGE (1808-1884) was a rich merchant in St.Petersburg, and son MIKHAIL (1838-1910), after service with Imperial Guards, became academician of painting. 1865 he toured Scotland and stayed with his cousins in Carluke, Dundee and Elgin. {RBC; RNL, f.144}.

YERMOLOV [Ермолов], MIKHAIL ALEXANDROVICH (1794-1850). Fought in French wars. 1825 resigned as colonel and went abroad. 1827 visited Scotland and at Abbotsford met Scott with whom he discussed literature and French invasion of Russia. 1829 promoted to major-gen., but took up writing. 1845 his article on Pushkin appeared in "Blackwood's Edinburgh Magazine". {Alexeyev, pp.292-3, 328, 355, 380-1}.

YUILLE, YULE [Ю(и)ль], PETER. Ca. 1615 officer in Russian army. {RIB, XXVIII}.

ROBERT Y. (1786-1861, Glasgow). Born into poor Scots family in Ireland. Worked as weaver and attended lectures at Glasgow and London. 1819 married Martha Cowie and joined W.Swan at Selenginsk Christian mission to the Buriats near Lake Baikal. 1840 mission was closed, and Y. left Russia. His Siberian diaries survive. {RNL, MSS, f.949, Nos.21-4; Bawden, Shamans, Lamas and Evangelicals}.

ZELENKO [Зеленко], ALEXANDER. Architect. 1901 assisted F.Shekhtel in his work for Glasgow International Exhibition. {SSR, No.10, 1988, p.183}.

ZINOVIEV [Зиновьев], VASILY NIKOLAYEVICH (1754-1822). Diplomat, author and freemason. President of Medical College. Related to Vorontsovs, Dashkovs and Orlovs. 1786 visited Edinburgh and Glasgow, met J.Watt, A.Smith, W.Robertson and J.Rogerson. In his journal admired Edinburgh's University and New Town (but not Old) and Scottish legal system. {RS, XXIII, 1878, pp.433-7}.

ZVERAKA (ZVEREV) [Зверака,(Зверев)], EVSTAFY FIODOROVICH (1751-1829, Kishinev). Son of Ukrainian priest. Sent to Britain to study agriculture under J.Arbuthnot, but chose medicine and went to Edinburgh where he stayed with Dashkovs 1778. 1779 got his M.D. from St.Andrews; elected hon. member of Edinburgh Physical Society. On return held medical posts in St.Petersburg, Elizavetgrad, Nikolayev and Kishinev. {RBS, ZH-Z, p.321; Cross, By the Banks, pp.62-6, 70, 136-7, 140}.

ZYBIN [Зыбин], VASILY. 1780-1 studied at Edinburgh University under Prof.Bruce, Fergusson, Blair and Robison. Back home he was regarded as a freak who pretended to have forgotten Russian and scorned the ignorance of his compatriots. {M.I.Pyliayev. Zamechatelnyye chudaki i originaly. St.Petersburg, 1898, pp.225-6}.